CASQUE D'OR

The French Film Guides
Series Editor: Ginette Vincendeau

From the pioneering days of the Lumière brothers' Cinématographe in 1895, France has been home to perhaps the most consistently vibrant film culture in the world, producing world-class directors and stars, and a stream of remarkable movies, from popular genre films to cult avant-garde works. Many of these have found a devoted audience outside France, and the arrival of DVD is now enabling a whole new generation to have access to contemporary titles as well as the great classics of the past.

    The French Film Guides build on this welcome new access, offering authoritative and entertaining guides to some of the most significant titles, from the silent era to the early 21st century. Written by experts in French cinema, the books combine extensive research with the author's distinctive, sometimes provocative perspective on each film. The series will thus build up an essential collection on great French classics, enabling students, teachers and lovers of French cinema both to learn more about their favourite films and make new discoveries in one of the world's richest bodies of cinematic work.

Ginette Vincendeau

Published French Film Guides:
Alphaville (Jean-Luc Godard, 1965) – Chris Darke
Amélie (Jean-Pierre Jeunet, 2001) – Isabelle Vanderschelden
Casque d'or (Jacques Becker, 1952) – Sarah Leahy
Cléo de 5 à 7 (Agnès Varda, 1961) – Valerie Orpen
Le Corbeau (Henri-Georges Clouzot, 1943) – Judith Mayne
Les Diaboliques (Henri-Georges Clouzot, 1954) – Susan Hayward
La Haine (Mathieu Kassovitz, 1995) – Ginette Vincendeau
La Reine Margot (Patrice Chéreau, 1994) – Julianne Pidduck

CASQUE D'OR

(Jacques Becker, 1952)

Sarah Leahy

UNIVERSITY OF ILLINOIS PRESS
URBANA AND CHICAGO

This edition produced by joint arrangement of I.B.Tauris & Co.
and the University of Illinois Press, and is available for sale only in North America.
1 2 3 4 5 C P 5 4 3 2 1

University of Illinois Press
1325 S. Oak St.
Champaign, IL 61820-6903
www.press.uillinois.edu

I.B.Tauris & Co., Ltd.
6 Salem Road
London W2 4BU
www.ibtauris.com

Library of Congress Cataloging-in-Publication Data

Leahy, Sarah.
Casque d'or : Jacques Becker, 1952 / Sarah Leahy.
p. cm. -- (The French film guides)
Includes bibliographical references.
ISBN-13: 978-0-252-03219-6 (cloth : alk. paper)
ISBN-10: 0-252-03219-5 (cloth : alk. paper)
ISBN-13: 978-0-252-07472-1 (pbk. : alk. paper)
ISBN-10: 0-252-07472-6 (pbk. : alk. paper)
1. Casque d'or (Motion picture)
I. Title.
PN1997.C3528L42   2007
791.43'72--dc22   2006027334

Contents

For my family, Fergus, Delma and Ruth

Acknowledgements

I would like first of all to thank Philippa Brewster at I.B.Tauris and Ginette Vincendeau for giving me the opportunity to write this book, which was made possible by the generous leave provided by the Arts and Humanities Research Council and Northumbria University. I would also like to thank Ginette Vincendeau for her invaluable feedback on earlier drafts, and staff at the Bibliothèque du Film (BiFi) and Centre National de la Cinématographie (CNC) in Paris and the British Film Institute (BFI) in London for their help in accessing archival material and to the School of Modern Languages at Newcastle University for funding the illustrations.

Thanks are also due to Julie Gauchotte and Imad Labidi at Studio Canal for arranging permission for the reproduction of stills (all rights are held by Studio Canal) and to the School of Modern Languages at Newcastle University for funding the illustrations.

Many friends and colleagues have contributed to this book through their support and comments, especially Susan Hayward, who supervised the doctoral thesis that inspired this work, Malcolm Gee, Peter Hutchings, Rosie White, Elizabeth Anderson and Máire Cross. Barbara Lehin offered me encouragement, friendly criticism and a place to stay in Paris. My family and friends kept me on track – thanks also to them.

Note

All translations from the French are my own unless otherwise stated.

Synopsis

Casque d'or opens with a riverside scene: several rowing boats are approaching the riverbank. In one of the boats, a woman with golden hair holds the oars: she is Marie (Simone Signoret), and she is arguing with her irritable boyfriend, Roland (William Sabatier). Her friends in the other boats are aware of the tension between the two. They all enter a *guinguette* (a riverside café and dance hall), where customers look disapprovingly at them, for they are prostitutes and *apaches* – gang members. One of the men, Raymond (Raymond Bussières), recognises an old friend, Manda (Serge Reggiani), a carpenter fixing the stage with his boss, Danard (Gaston Modot). Marie, dancing reluctantly with Roland, spots Manda and seduces him with her gaze. Raymond introduces Manda to his friends, and Marie invites him to dance, much to Roland's displeasure.

The following morning, Marie is brought to see Félix Leca (Claude Dauphin), the gang leader. Leca offers to buy Marie from Roland. While Leca and his gang share out the proceeds of their recent bank robbery, Marie visits Manda, but discovers that he is engaged to Danard's daughter. That evening, the gang assembles at the Ange Gabriel, a café and dance hall. Marie agrees to Leca's offer, but then Manda arrives. There is a duel between Manda and Roland, and Roland is killed. Manda declines to join Leca's gang and escapes just before the police arrive.

The following morning, Manda receives a note from Raymond, asking him to meet at Mère Eugène's farm in Joinville. There he finds not Raymond, however, but Marie. The couple spend two blissful days together, before they 'run into' Leca, who lets Manda know that he can now safely return to Paris, since Raymond has been arrested for Roland's murder. Leca has framed Raymond, in an attempt to get Manda to give himself up and thus to win back Marie.

Manda disappears, and Marie, desperate for help, turns to Leca for help. Leca demands sexual favours from Marie in return for his help. Manda confesses to killing Roland, and encounters Raymond at the police station, who discovers Leca's treachery. Leca betrays Marie, who goes alone to the prison to help Manda and Raymond escape. They get away, but Raymond is severely wounded.

Manda now goes in search of Leca, but, at his house, finds only Marie's slippers – giving him a double reason for revenge. Eventually he tracks down his quarry, following him into the police station, cornering him in the courtyard and shooting him dead. The final sequence shows Marie watching over Manda's execution. As the blade falls, Marie's golden head bows, before the image dissolves to a final shot of the couple waltzing in the now empty *guinguette*.

Introduction

Casque d'or is now hailed in France as a *chef d'œuvre* of the classical cinema, though it is less well known internationally.[1] This is a reversal of the situation that greeted its release at home and abroad in 1952, when the French public and critics' decidedly lukewarm response was countered by international success: warm reviews and box office success in Britain, Italy and Germany and a British Academy Award for best actress for Simone Signoret in the title role. It is now seen as a showcase not just for its stars, Signoret, Serge Reggiani and Claude Dauphin, but also for some of the better-known 'second roles' of French cinema: Raymond Bussières and Gaston Modot, in particular. Indeed, in a 1979 poll of the French Academy of Cinematographic Arts and Techniques, taken to mark the fiftieth anniversary of the coming of sound, *Casque d'or* was voted third-best French film of all time, after *Les Enfants du paradis* (Carné, 1943–1945) and *La Grande illusion* (Renoir, 1937).[2]

The film is atypical in many ways: as a costume drama it differs from Becker's earlier films, known for their detailed depiction of contemporary life in different *milieux*, yet neither does it fit in with the trend for literary adaptations and lavish reconstructions of the past that characterised many of the 'quality tradition' films of the 1950s. The film's minimalist dialogue goes against the wordy literary tradition of 1950s screenwriting, dominated as it was by Henri Jeanson, Jean Aurenche and Pierre Bost. A gangster movie, it draws on the 1930s American cinema, yet it does not follow the typical rise and fall trajectory of the hero, instead using the very French tradition of the Belle Epoque *apaches* (urban bandits or gangsters) as the background to the love story between Marie and Manda. *Casque d'or* is now recognised for its 'authenticity', thanks to its setting among working and criminal classes, the realistic, understated performances of the cast, the use of location shooting and costumes that were uninfluenced by 1950s fashions. And yet, it does not conform to definitions of realism that dominated this time, transgressing by its melodramatic subject matter, use of studio sets, stars and well-known actors and, perhaps most notably, its use of continuity editing. To paraphrase Truffaut on Becker, it could be said to be 'at the opposite pole to every tendency in French cinema'.[3]

This study offers a detailed exploration of *Casque d'or's* position in French cinema, tracing its trajectory from box office flop to recognised classic, and arguing that this delayed recognition can be attributed to the fact that it is so different from the dominant French cinema of the 1950s – generically, aesthetically but most crucially in terms of its representations of class and gender. The first part will focus on the cinematic and cultural context of the film, looking at how it fits into the careers of Jacques Becker and its stars, as well as examining the film in relation to the traditions and tendencies of French cinema. This part also offers analysis of Becker's sources, including an in-depth discussion of the story of Amélie Hélie, the real Casque d'or. The second part looks in more detail at the film itself, examining narrative structure, the question of realism, stardom and performance and addressing the representation of class and gender. The final part looks at the film's reception both at home and abroad and at the critical legacy of *Casque d'or*.

Notes

1   This situation may be somewhat rectified by the recent DVD release of the film in the USA.
2   Andrew, Dudley, *Mists of Regret: Culture and Sensibility in Classic French Film* (Princeton: Princeton University Press, 1995), fn. 1, p. 386.
3   Truffaut, François, 'The rogues are weary', in Jim Hillier (ed.), *Cahiers du Cinéma: The 1950s – Neo-realism, Hollywood, New Wave* (Cambridge, MA: Harvard University Press, 1985), pp. 28–29.

1   Production contexts

Jacques Becker: the director

Jacques Becker (1906–1960) is one of a generation of film-makers (which also includes Henri-Georges Clouzot, Robert Bresson and Yves Allégret) whose careers took off during the Second World War, and who would go on to be among the leading film-makers of 1950s France. Becker was to make a total of 13 feature films, before his career was cut short by his premature death in 1960 at the age of 54. *Casque d'or* is the seventh of these films, and occupies a central position in more ways than one within the *œuvre* of its director. As we shall see, this film can be seen as the meeting point of all the primary themes that recur throughout Becker's work: the heterosexual couple and its position within society, male friendship with its concomitant aspects of loyalty and betrayal, depiction of the group and of specific *milieux*. There is not enough space here to give a full account of Becker's career, so we will concentrate on the films he made leading up to *Casque d'or*, though some attention will also be given to his later work.

Jacques Becker was born in Paris in 1906 into a bourgeois, Protestant family. His father was from Lorraine and his mother of Scottish and Irish descent, and Becker was brought up to be bilingual.[1] Becker grew up with a passion for music, especially jazz, for motor cars and engines, and for cinema. In 1925, he took a job on a transatlantic liner, where he met King Vidor and persuaded him to take him on as an assistant. Becker's father put a stop to this plan, requiring him to return home to a 'serious' job with the Fulmen engineering firm. Becker's engineering career would not last long, though: in 1932 he resigned, determined to take his chances as an assistant director to his friend, Jean Renoir.

Early career

Becker, like many of his contemporaries, served a long apprenticeship, working with Renoir from 1932–1938, on almost all his films from *La Nuit du carrefour* to *La Marseillaise* as 'creative collaborator' as much as assistant director.[2] Becker enjoyed a close professional and personal connection with Renoir, whose influence can be seen in Becker's films, which share Renoir's fondness for his characters and a concern with 'authenticity'. Becker and Renoir also shared a political commitment to the French Communist Party (PCF) during the mid-1930s. Though Becker's connection to the PCF was to wane in the post-war period, he remained a committed man of the Left, and many of his later films, not least *Casque d'or*, draw on a left-wing celebratory mythology of the working classes and popular cultural icons in order to achieve their celebrated 'authenticity'.

During his apprenticeship, Becker made a couple of short films of his own, financed by a schoolfriend, André Halley des Fontaines: *Le Commissaire est bon enfant* (co-directed with Pierre Prévert, 1935) and *Une tête qui rapporte* (1935). However, Becker's partnership with both Renoir and Halley des Fontaines was interrupted by a dispute over *Sur la cour*, a script by Jean Castanyer that would become *Le Crime de Monsieur Lange* (1935). Castanyer had originally approached Becker to direct the film, but Halley des Fontaines offered the script to the more experienced Renoir, who rewrote it with Jacques Prévert. Becker considered this lack of faith a betrayal by his two closest friends, but he would return to the Renoir fold the following year, playing a leading role on the set of the PCF-funded *La Vie est à nous* (1936). When Becker and Halley des Fontaines found themselves in the same prisoner-of-war camp in 1941, they too put their differences behind them, and this childhood friend went on to produce two out of Becker's first three films (*Dernier atout* and *Falbalas*).

Before embarking on his career as director, Becker was to work once again as an assistant, this time to Albert Valentin on *L'Héritier des Mondésir*, starring Fernandel and filmed in Berlin in 1939 prior to the outbreak of war, but released in 1940. He then made a false start on his career as director of *L'Or du Cristobal*, which was interrupted during filming due to a financial dispute between Becker and the producers. The film was eventually finished by Jean Stelli and Becker always refused to recognise it.

Becker was beginning to make his mark as a director, then, when war broke out. Captured in 1941, he remained a prisoner of war for a year, before returning to France and embarking seriously on his film career. He made his first three feature films under the Occupation: *Dernier atout* (1942), *Goupi*

Mains Rouges (1943) and *Falbalas* (1944, released in 1945). Though Becker refused to work for the German-owned Continental, he formed an acquaintanceship with Lucien Rebatet, the influential fascist film critic for *Je suis partout* (who wrote under the name of François Vinneuil). According to Claude Naumann, Becker thought Rebatet a perceptive and sensitive critic, though he disagreed vehemently with his fascist and anti-Semitic views. Becker's attitude towards Rebatet could be seen as evidence of the same broad-minded attitude that would later enable him to use his position on the Comité de Libération du Cinéma Français (CLCF) to speak up for journalists like Rebatet and film-makers like Clouzot, even though he disapproved of their political positions, because he felt they were bearing the brunt of the purges while politicians got off lightly. Of course, it is also true that cultivating an acquaintanceship with such an influential figure could only be of benefit to an ambitious film-maker embarking on his career, and indeed, as Naumann describes, Rebatet's reviews of Becker's Occupation films were often favourable.[3] Becker's political sympathies, however, lay with the Communist Resistance: he employed Resistance fighters such as Max Douy (set designer on *Dernier atout*) and Nicolas Hayer (cinematographer on *Dernier atout* and *Falbalas*), and encouraged clandestine activity on the sets of *Dernier atout* and *Falbalas* – Hayer began making a documentary that was to become *La Libération de Paris* (1944) while working on *Falbalas*. Becker was extremely ambitious personally but he was also committed to the good of the French film industry. He was known for his support of colleagues such as Bresson and Max Ophüls, and, later on, for the young directors of the New Wave. Becker was a cinephile, who developed his conception of cinema in articles for *L'Ecran français* and *Arts* as well as in his films. This attitude earned him the admiration of the establishment and also of the young critics of the *Cahiers du cinéma* and he was hailed as an *auteur* by both camps.

The films

Dernier atout, the first full-length feature film that Becker recognised, was received by critics as a well-crafted but slight film – evidence of a new cinematic talent. It was also welcomed by a public deprived of the American films it emulated. A gangster film set in a fictional South American country (though filmed in and around Nice), *Dernier atout* is a light, fast-paced thriller with witty, bantering dialogue. It tells the story of Montès (Georges Rollin) and Clarence (Raymond Rouleau), two trainee policemen – rivals for the top spot – who are set the task of finding out who murdered a notorious gangster on holiday from Chicago, and who become involved with the mysterious and beautiful Bella (Mireille Balin). Also featuring Pierre Renoir, Noël Roquevert and Gaston Modot, the film sketches out some of the major themes that Becker's later films would explore in greater depth: masculine friendship and betrayal, and the relationship between the individual and the group.

It was Becker's second film, *Goupi Mains Rouges* (1943), that put the spotlight on him as one of the most important directors to emerge during this period, and nowadays, along with *Le Corbeau* (Clouzot, 1943) and *Les Visiteurs du soir* (Carné, 1942), it is often hailed as one of the most important films of the Occupation. The film reveals the rivalries and jealousy of a close-knit peasant family, who nonetheless band together when faced with the outside interference of a police murder investigation. It featured Fernand Ledoux and Robert Le Vigan alongside Blanchette Brunoy and Georges Rollin.

Goupi Mains Rouges was highly praised for its ambitious narrative centred on the Goupi clan, and for the authenticity with which the characters and their *milieu* are portrayed. Location shooting on a farm in the Charente in the South-West of France, the use of real costumes borrowed from locals, the fleshing out of secondary characters via gesture and *mise-en-scène* rather than dialogue all contribute to this 'authenticity' and reveal elements of Becker's style that we will find in later films. And again, we see Becker's favourite themes emerging: portrayal of the group and its *milieu*; the couple and their relationship to the group; and, of course, the privileging of character development over plot.

Falbalas, Becker's next film, depicts the world of the brilliant designer Philippe Clarence (Raymond Rouleau) and those who work for him. Filmed under the Occupation, *Falbalas* was not released until after the Liberation. The film once again features questions of betrayal and masculine friendship, but the main female character is much more developed than in Becker's previous two films. Micheline (Micheline Presle) is engaged to Daniel, a close friend and business associate of Clarence. When Clarence meets Micheline he offers to design her wedding dress, but then sets about seducing her. She becomes his muse, and he is inspired to re-create his entire collection. However, when Clarence breaks off their affair, Micheline refuses to 'play the game' and confronts his hypocrisy. Clarence, eventually realising that he is in love with Micheline, attempts to win her back. However, she turns him down, and Clarence, driven mad by his obsession, throws himself out of the window, embracing a mannequin that bears a striking resemblance to Micheline. *Falbalas* is unusual for its time in its serious treatment of female desire through the character of Micheline, a thoroughly 'modern' young woman, especially because she ends the film alone by her own choice, and not as a punishment for her 'transgressive' behaviour.

Such characters would feature strongly in Becker's next three films, made after the Liberation: indeed, from *Falbalas* to *Casque d'or* there is a strong focus on female characters who take the initiative, which is missing from Becker's later work. *Antoine et Antoinette* (1947) was his first post-war project. Co-written with Françoise Giroud,[4] the film focuses on an 'ordinary' working-class couple. The deliberately slim plotline, featuring a misplaced winning lottery ticket, allows the film to concentrate on developing the characters and portraying the environment in which they live. As with the earlier *Goupi* and *Falbalas*, Becker was concerned with the authenticity of his characters and their *milieu*. His use of relatively little-known actors for his leads (Claire Maffei and Roger Pigaut) and the working-class setting led to the film being hailed as the French answer to Italian neo-realism, although the film arguably draws more closely on the comedies of René Clair (notably *Le Million*, 1931) and American screwball comedies such as *His Girl Friday* (Hawks, 1940) than on *Bicycle Thieves* (de Sica, 1945) or *Rome, open city* (Rossellini, 1945). Becker's concern for secondary roles can be seen in characters such as Antoinette's friend Juliette (Antoinette Poivre), who sells tickets in the Metro, the young boxer who is the couple's neighbour (Pierre Trabaud) and especially the greengrocer, played by Noël Roquevert, who can be seen as a forerunner of the lecherous Leca in *Casque d'or*. Here we remain in the realm of comedy, so Antoinette is able to resist the vile *épicier*'s advances whereas Marie must use her body as currency in order to try and obtain what she wants (Manda's freedom). Though some critics decried the slimness of the plot, *Antoine et Antoinette* was once again a critical and popular success for Becker, and won him the prize for Best Film at the Cannes Film Festival of 1947.

Becker pursued the 'neo-realist' vein, casting unknown beginners along-side more established actors in his next film, *Rendez-vous de juillet*, which focuses on a group of young friends in Saint Germain-des-Prés. More than any of Becker's other films, *Rendez-vous de juillet* celebrates the jazz music that he loved so much. However, the narrative, set loosely around a young anthropologist's attempts to put together an expedition to carry out research into the Pygmy tribe, and the various efforts of his friends to succeed in their chosen fields, is rather weak, and the somewhat stilted dialogue lacks the authenticity that Becker hoped to impart to his young characters. That said, *Rendez-vous de juillet* can be said to anticipate the New Wave as one of the few films of the decade that focuses on the everyday existence of young people, and because it featured so many newcomers: Maurice Ronet, Brigitte Auber and Nicole Courcel in their first roles, and Daniel Gélin in his first leading part. The film received a poor critical reception when it was presented at Cannes in 1949, and although it was awarded the Louis Delluc prize, it marked the beginning of a decline in his critical currency. With the possible exception of *Touchez pas au grisbi*, none of his future films would achieve the immediate critical success of his early career.

Edouard et Caroline (1951) is no exception to this – it was vilified by much of the press as a film that wasted its carefully crafted *mise-en-scène* on an unworthy plot, and by left-wingers such as Georges Sadoul as confirmation that Becker had abandoned the working classes. The script, co-written with Annette Wademant, Becker's partner at this time, emulates American screwball comedies, and the film was shot entirely in studios to a very tight schedule. A misplaced waistcoat and an altered evening gown are the pretexts for a row that threatens Edouard and Caroline's marriage and which foregrounds the class difference between them. The sequences set at Caroline's uncle's house offer a satirical look at the leisured classes. Though the film ends with a passionate reconciliation, the couple's marriage is not the happily-ever-after Hollywood variety: we are left with the distinct impression that this will be a recurring pattern in their relationship!

The film which followed *Casque d'or*, *Rue de l'Estrapade* (1953), would be the last to put the emphasis on the heterosexual couple. With *Touchez pas au grisbi*, Becker moved towards the depiction of a more masculine universe, one sketched out first in *Dernier atout*, and then in *Casque d'or* in the friendship between Manda and Raymond and in Leca's gang. The *milieu* so carefully re-created in these three films allows Becker to pay homage to American cinema (most particularly in *Dernier atout*), but he is also credited with creating a specifically French version of the genre with *Touchez pas au grisbi*, opening the way for films such as *Du Rififi chez les hommes* (Dassin, 1955) and *Bob le flambeur* (Melville, 1955). These films featuring older, tired gangsters were extremely popular with 1950s audiences (*Grisbi* gave Jean Gabin's flagging career a much-needed boost), and offered a contrast to the parodic thrillers such as *Méfiéz-vous des blondes* (Hunebelle, 1950 – starring Raymond Rouleau building on his role in *Dernier atout*), or the Lemmy Caution series starring Eddie Constantine as the whisky-drinking, womanising FBI agent, launched with *La Môme Vert-de-gris* (Borderie, 1953).

Becker would return to costume drama twice in his later career: once again to the Belle Epoque with *Les Aventures d'Arsène Lupin* (1957) – described by Bazin as a sort of comic remake of *Casque d'or*[5] – and to the 1920s with *Montparnasse 19* (1958) – a project based on the life of Modigliani that Becker inherited from Max Ophüls, who died during the preparation of the film. However, the themes that he would continue to explore in his later films, such as loyalty, betrayal and masculine friendship (*Casque d'or, Touchez pas au grisbi, Le Trou*), the artist/artisan and the act of creation (*Montparnasse 19* but also *Casque d'or* and even *Le Trou*), are already present in his earlier films. Indeed, *Casque d'or* can be seen as a transitional film in which all Becker's themes meet. Let us now turn to the inspiration for the subject matter with which the film addresses these concerns: the real Casque d'or and Becker's other sources.

The real Casque d'or and other sources

Casque d'or was inspired by a *fait divers* that caused a scandal throughout Paris in 1902, when Amélie Hélie, known as 'Casque d'or' (on account of the 'helmet' of golden hair she wore piled on top of her head), and the *apaches* (a term imported from the USA by journalists inspired by the adventure novels of Gustave Aimard)[6] appeared on the front pages of newspapers such as *Le Petit parisien* and *Le Matin*, as well as in the court reports of *Le Figaro*. However, Hélie's tale is not the only inspiration for Becker's film. In spite of the wealth of information that exists about *Casque d'or* and its genesis, there is no record of the actual sources that Becker used in the elaboration of his final script in 1951. Although the story of the film is very different from that of the real Casque d'or and her rival lovers Manda and Leca, there are certain elements of the film that lead us to suppose that Becker was either familiar with the events and used them as a loose inspiration for his script, or that he drew on earlier versions of scripts that were based more closely on the *fait divers*.

Becker did comment on some sources of inspiration, especially *Petit illustré* – a publication aimed principally at children that specialised in reporting the more sensational criminal events, complete with artists' impressions of the characters and places involved.[7] There is an aspect of the film that could be said to come from a kind certain popular imagination of the Parisian *faubourgs* in the Belle Epoque – an imagination that draws on anarchist and left-wing mythologies. This is also connected to cinematic influences on Becker, such as the crime series of Feuillade or even the 1930s films of Renoir or Carné and Prévert, which will be discussed in a later section (*Casque d'or* and French cinema). We will now turn to the real Casque d'or, in order to see how Becker transformed her story for the screen, before looking at these popular cultural influences.

Hélie's story is quite different from the one Becker elaborated in his film. Born in Orléans in 1879, she was crowned 'Queen of the *Apaches*' in 1902 by the sensationalist press. Hélie was already working as a prostitute when she met Manda in 1898. Hélie claims that they were in love, but makes it clear that he also profited from her activities. The drama that led to her fame began at Christmas 1901, when she left Manda and moved in with François Leca, head of the Popincourt *apaches*, provoking a war between the two rival gangs. Various skirmishes and battles led to Leca being seriously wounded. Believing he was about to die, he denounced Manda, who was arrested and tried for attempted murder in May of 1902. Hélie appeared as a prosecution witness, but throughout her testimony remained loyal to her former lover. Manda received a life sentence of hard labour in a penal colony, and, according to Lanoux, did well in prison, ending up in charge of the infirmary.[8] Leca, meanwhile, had survived his injuries and faced trial in turn in October 1902, accused of various offences. He was sentenced to eight years' hard labour and died in prison in French Guyana.

Amélie Hélie's notoriety grew during 1902, fed by rival newspapers. She appeared in a play entitled *Casque d'or and the Apaches* at the Théâtre des Bouffes du Nord. Her portrait was painted by Albert Dupré and destined for exhibition at the Salon. (Both play and portrait were censored by the Prefect, Lépine, horrified at the apparent acceptance by the bourgeoisie of this common prostitute.) After Manda's trial, however, she soon sank into obscurity. Prevented from working as a prostitute by the authorities and unable to go on the stage, she found work for a while in the circus with a masked lion-tamer (a show Lépine also did his best to close). She was attacked and stabbed by one of Manda's faithful gang members, seeking vengeance on the woman he believed had denounced his chief. Hélie recovered from her wounds, and eventually met and married André Nardin, not a carpenter but a varnisher from Bagnolet, a district not so far removed from those that had witnessed her earlier exploits. Hélie lived out the remainder of her days in quiet respectability, and died in 1933 from tuberculosis.

Amélie Hélie's story is remarkable for several reasons. Firstly, the reporting of her presence at Manda's trial reveals the double standards existing in French society throughout the nineteenth and early twentieth centuries. Such trials threatened the protection of 'honest' bourgeois women from the venality of prostitution and the corruption of sexuality. As *Le Figaro* reported:

> The publicity surrounding the whore Amélie Hélie – falsely known as Casque d'or – ensured a scandalously overcrowded courtroom yesterday. Women who were not all from her milieu heaved, pushed and squeezed their way in to catch a glimpse of three pimps in the dock and a prostitute in the courtroom. And how ordinary she is! For a start she doesn't have as much hair as they say. She combs and teases it and wears it very low on her forehead underneath her large hat – that's all.[9]

This demystification of Hélie – in particular the criticism of her famous hair – suggests that she was a threatening character, seen as transgressing the boundary between 'honest' women and those of her station. We must remember that prostitution was seen by many nineteenth-century moralists as a necessity to protect the virtue of bourgeois women. This is one reason that explains Prefect Lépine's determination to limit her exposure.

Secondly, Hélie's own attitude was far from the demure deferral before authority that was expected of women of her class. She is often depicted defiantly smoking a cigarette, an insolent smile on her face.[10] While Hélie's lack of solidarity with her fellow prostitutes might preclude her from becoming a feminist icon, she does nonetheless offer a rare public glimpse of an unashamed sexuality, outside of the realm of the cabaret. And, more than this, she took control of her own story, playing the papers' game in order to publicise herself. Alain Corbin points to the fact that the little information that we have regarding the lives of prostitutes at this time is brought to us not by the women themselves but by the authorities who regulated them: 'The nineteenth century prostitute does not speak to us about herself; what reality we can glean is mediated through male eyes: those of the policeman, the doctor, the judge, and the administrator.'[11] Hélie, however, takes every opportunity to recount her life, first on stage, then in court, and then in the weekly paper *Fin de siècle*. Hélie's story, 'told in her own words', is featured on the front page in several weekly instalments between June and August 1902.[12]

Hélie's tale reveals some important aspects of the life of an independent prostitute, a type rapidly taking over from the *fille de maison* at this time, and perceived as more threatening by the authorities because of the greater difficulties involved in regulation.[13] She would solicit on the street in summer but would spend winter working in a brothel, though not as an inmate. Hélie has been depicted by some as an over-ambitious *femme fatale* who soon forgot her lovers when fortune smiled on her.[14] However, given her situation and the fact that both Manda and Leca could perhaps more accurately be described as pimps than lovers, it is hardly surprising that she should wish to exploit a bourgeois fascination with the 'lower depths'.

Though Becker's characters are quite different, he has retained certain aspects, such as the code of honour of the *milieu* – where rival gangs would fight and even kill each other, and yet would close ranks when confronted with the law. Names of characters, especially nicknames, are recycled – le Dénicheur (the Bird-nester), le Boulanger (the Baker) – as well as surnames, such as Manda, Leca and Ponsard. Marie's insolent, ironic smile and her way of lighting up a cigarette to signify that she couldn't care less what Roland thinks are close to the written descriptions and the pictures of Amélie Hélie. Becker has, however, taken certain liberties with the appearance of his Casque d'or: Signoret's hair is blonde rather than the golden-red of the original (platinum blond is much more striking in a black and white film) and is piled more tightly on top of her head than Amélie Hélie's was. Pictures of Hélie show her wearing blouses and dresses that button up to the neck – quite different from the plunging necklines of Signoret's blouses, which slip temptingly off her shoulder during her meeting with Leca. Reggiani bears the moustache and cap sported by many *apaches* of the period, but in Becker's film these have been reclaimed as emblems of the working class.[15] The real Manda, like most of the *apaches*, was linked to a trade even if he did not practise it much (according to Lanoux he was a polisher) and this is the case for Raymond 'le Boulanger' in Becker's film.

Armand Lanoux's version of the story of Casque d'or, published in 1958 as part of the 'true story' of the Third Republic, is particularly interesting in the way it draws for imagery if not for events on Becker's film, demonstrating how history and fiction eventually blur to create a legend. He also insists on the fact that Manda/the Man was an honest worker who turned to the bad after meeting Amélie.[16] Indeed, the existence of Becker's film must surely be one important reason why the otherwise forgotten anecdote of Casque d'or is included in this volume at all.

Becker's film also draws in a wider sense on the popular imagination that adopted Casque d'or as a legend of the *faubourgs*. This is the cultural realm of the songs of Aristide Bruant, the stories and images recounted in *Petit illustré* about anarchist attacks and the legendary Bonnot gang,[17] the writing of Eugène Sue and the paintings of Renoir. Becker claimed that he gained inspiration for the pictorial side of his film from *Petit illustré* and not from Toulouse Lautrec or Manet.[18] However, there are clear parallels between the rural sequences at the *guinguette*, for example, and Pierre Auguste Renoir's paintings, some filtered via Jean Renoir's *Une Partie de campagne*, on which Becker worked as an assistant in 1936. Paintings that we could cite include *Dance at Bougival* (1882–1883), *Dance in the country* (1882–1883) and *The Luncheon of the Boating Party* (1880–1881), which relate particularly to the scenes at the *guinguette* and the Ange Gabriel. Marie's silent approach towards the sleeping Manda on the Joinville riverbank recalls *The Rowing Boat* (1878–1880), which depicts a solitary woman dressed in white approaching the shore in a boat, while *Woman Reading* (c. 1876) and *Young Woman braiding her Hair* (1876) anticipate Signoret's hairstyles in the film.[19] Dudley Andrew has also remarked upon this similarity – especially with regard to the setting: 'Rowboats, dancers, drinking boatmen, trellised dance floors, and a riverside setting certify the reference to the great painter.' However, it is not only visually that Becker draws on Renoir – the mixture of social classes in these scenes is also reminiscent of these paintings, where the bourgeoisie share their leisure spaces with prostitutes and workers.[20]

If the more rural sequences draw on Renoir, the overall plot recalls the songs of Aristide Bruant, which mythologised the underclasses in tales where both love and life are cheap – songs such as *A la Villette*, the lament of a *grisette* (a 'working girl') for her young lover whom she lost to the guillotine:

> He was a bit rough in all his ways
> But still he was a handsome lad
> He was the best-looking, he was one of the best
> At la Villette
>
> …
>
> He loved me and I loved him
> We'd never have left each other
> If there'd never been the police
> At la Villette
>
> …
>
> The last time that I saw him
> His chest it was stripped bare
> And his head held fast in the *lunette*
> At la Roquette.[21]

Bruant's songs poeticised marginal Paris – what Rudorff refers to as 'the sad wasteland of the outer boulevards and fortifications'.[22] Arguably, *Casque d'or* has also borrowed from Bruant a certain directness of style, transforming the authenticity of language of the songs into one of images, combining humour with tragedy and a sense of solidarity with the subjects of the stories, be they *apache*, prostitute or beggar.

This style is also drawn from *Le Petit illustré*, first published in 1904. This children's paper – also popular with many adults of the lower classes – abandoned the didactic tone adopted by most of the children's press for a more entertaining style, often incorporating crude humour and slang. It was also very cheap to buy, and featured illustrated versions of frequently bloody and notorious *fait divers*, such as the downfall of Bonnot's gang, as well as fictional stories.[23] The 1969 film *La Bande à Bonnot* (Philippe Fourastié) draws on similar imagery and sources as *Casque d'or*, using illustrations from *Le Petit Illustré* for the opening credits, which are played to the tune of *Le Temps des cerises*, Jean-Baptiste Clément's song of lost youth and love that became an anthem of the Commune – a left-wing riposte to the Right's appropriation of the Marseillaise during the 1930s, which features at the end of *Casque d'or*.[24] *Le Petit illustré* has accumulated its own mythology, thanks to celebrations of popular literature in films such as *Le Crime de Monsieur Lange* (Renoir, 1936), but also to the reproduction of its illustrations in all sorts of publications, from Guilleminault's *Le Roman vrai de la Troisième République* (1958) to the 1999 Gaumont DVD edition of Feuillade's *Fantômas*, which offers some of the more lurid stories as an extra. Becker cites this paper from his childhood as the principal source of inspiration for the caped policemen and the Paris streets that feature in *Casque d'or*.

These references were missed however in 1952 and this stylised aspect of both image and dialogue was dismissed as clichéd and over-simplistic at the time of *Casque d'or*'s release – a time when scriptwriters were celebrated in French cinema. From a twenty-first-century perspective, though, it links the film more closely with the popular cultural realm of the 'ordinary' people – a tradition including Bruant, both Renoirs (father and son) and, indeed, Amélie Hélie herself. Perhaps the strength of this cultural tradition is one reason why Hélie's story attracted so much interest from film-makers from the 1930s onwards. Let us now turn to an examination of the evolution of the *Casque d'or* film project from the early pre-war scripts to Becker's 1952 film.

Project, cast and crew

Simone Signoret describes *Casque d'or* as having been filmed in an atmosphere of 'love, joy, friendship and humour'.[25] Even if *Casque d'or* is recognised as a *film d'auteur*, it is, like all films, a collective achievement, as Signoret's description emphasises. Many of those involved (Becker, Bussières, Modot, Reggiani, Houllé-Renoir, Signoret) were committed men and women of the Left, some connected with the legendary Groupe Octobre, or with Renoir's 1930s film-making team. Indeed, *Casque d'or* had been around as a film project since before the war, when Julien Duvivier had planned to make it with Jean Gabin as Manda and a script by Henri Jeanson. The fact, then, that the film was not made until 1951 is highly significant, as Susan Hayward has pointed out.[25] Becker's 1951 script is radically different from either Hélie's story, as we have seen, or from earlier scenarios. This section will argue that the evolution of the project into the film we know was shaped by both the historical context and the cast and crew involved.

A project with a history

Becker had written a script for *Casque d'or* in 1946, along with Maurice Griffe and Roger Vitrac. However, work was abandoned when Duvivier opposed the new project. The producing team of the Hakim brothers eventually won the right to make the film, which was offered to Clouzot and then Yves Allégret. In 1951, Becker approached producers Robert Hakim and Michel Safra, offering himself as director. Financial constraints meant he had to entirely rewrite the film, this time calling in Jacques Companeez to help out. It was Companeez who came up with the idea that Leca should betray Raymond in order to push Manda into giving himself up.[27]

If the Jeanson script was ever written, it is now untraceable. However, there is an earlier scenario, written by André Paul Antoine, in which Casque d'or (still called Amélie in this version) is painted in a very different light.[28] Encouraged by journalists hungry for stories, she deliberately foments trouble between a violent Manda and a gullible Leca in order to maximise her own celebrity. The ending sees the reconciliation of the two rivals, who meet up in the same penal colony. Casque d'or, however, does not profit from her brief moment of fame, and the final scene would have her as a fat old woman trying to make a living by selling a handful of grubby laces to passers-by.

Becker's 1946 version takes more liberties with Hélie's story. Casque d'or starts out as Leca's mistress but pursues Manda, forcing him to leave Leca's gang and set up his own rival band of *apaches*. She is a manipulative *femme fatale* who embodies desire and greed – a far cry from the Marie embodied by Simone Signoret. Becker also introduced a new character, Monsieur Benoît, to be played by Louis Jouvet.[29] Benoît, encountered by chance at the beginning of the film, rows Manda across to the *guinguette* on the opposite bank, where he will become embroiled in a fight and end up killing a man. The two men become friends, without knowing what the other does for a living, and only at the end is it revealed that Benoît is the executioner. Valérie Vignaux, author of a monograph on Becker, points out the heavy fatalism of this character, associated firmly with the pessimistic pre-war cinematic vein, where fate weighs heavy on the doomed hero.[30] Like these pre-war films, a much greater emphasis is placed on the male characters and Casque d'or is sidelined: even the final image of her watching over Manda's execution loses its power and poignancy since she is so tainted by self-interest.

The 1951 script, even if it is a tragedy, has moved away from this fatalistic pessimism, completely transforming the main characters and the plot. Manda and Marie are now the central characters with Leca, the villain, also featuring prominently.[31] Marie and Manda are now fundamentally good, avoiding cinematic clichés such as the 'garce' (bitch), or the doomed hero. Even Leca is a more developed character. More importantly, this version has abandoned the pre-war obsession with masculinity in crisis to focus on contemporary issues such as sexual equality and corruption in public life, as well as referring to France's recent history through Leca's double-dealing and denunciations. And yet, though the film was praised for its realistic re-creation of Belleville in the Belle Epoque (in spite of the liberties Becker had taken with the original story), it was not perceived in terms of its contemporary relevance – indeed, it was associated more readily with the pre-war cinematic sensibility.

Cast and crew: a film 'collective'

One aspect that could lead to this association is the cast of *Casque d'or*. Regarded almost universally as a great strength of the film because of the interaction between actors as well as individual performances, it is also the case that many members were veterans of Renoir's 1930s films, or of the Groupe Octobre, the 1930s left-wing theatre group led by the poet and scriptwriter Jacques Prévert. Foremost among these is Raymond Bussières. Though he had not worked with Becker prior to *Casque d'or*, he was known to the director as a founder member of the Groupe Octobre, which also included Gaston Modot. Modot was a veteran of four of Renoir's films: *La Vie est à nous* – in the sketch directed by Becker; *La Grande illusion*; *La Marseillaise*; and – the only one on which Becker did not work – *La Règle du jeu*. Modot also worked with Becker on *Antoine et Antoinette, Rendez-vous de juillet*. Loleh Bellon (Léonie Danard) was also connected with both the Groupe Octobre and Renoir through her uncle, critic and actor Jacques Brunius. Becker had also worked previously with Tony Corteggiani (the Commissaire), Emile Genevois (Billy), Yette Lucas (Mère Adèle), and Paul Barge (Inspector Juliani). It was not uncommon for directors to build teams of actors, almost like a repertory group, indeed the structure of the French film industry lent itself to such practices. However, Becker's use of so many actors who had such close bonds with each other for *Casque d'or* clearly draws on Renoir's 1930s vision of film-making as a collective practice – a practice that nurtured Becker – and permits even those playing minor roles to invest them with an extraordinary level of humanity.

Casque d'or differs from Becker's other films with respect to continuity of principal actors. In his other films he 'recycled' actors such as Georges Rollin, Daniel Gélin, Anne Vernon and Raymond Rouleau from film to film. In *Casque d'or*, this continuity is provided by the 'second roles', as we have seen, whereas the starring roles were new to Becker. The director stated in

1954 that Manda was already Reggiani for him in 1946.[32] However, Daniel Gélin – a favourite actor of Becker's – claims that he was offered the role in 1951, but that the offer was withdrawn due to poor relations with Becker's partner, Annette Wademant.[33] Reggiani's name appears on all documentation in the production archive, so Gélin cannot have figured seriously as a candidate for the role for long. On the other hand, production documents show that the part of Leca was initially destined for Franck Villard, best known for his roles in *Gigi* (Audry, 1948) and as Signoret's con-man lover in *Manèges* (Yves Allégret, 1950). However, Becker eventually turned to the older and more established Claude Dauphin to play the part. As for Signoret, it seems that she was the first choice for the character of Marie once Becker picked up the project again in 1951, and it is possible that her star image influenced the writing of this version that makes Marie a much more prominent character. Even before *Casque d'or* Signoret was credited with achieving a depth of characterisation that transcended the old stereotypes of the 'garce' (bitch) or the 'tart' (Signoret's own descriptions).[34] However, even after signing the contract, Signoret almost backed out of the film at the last minute in order to spend more time with Montand on the set of *Le Salaire de la peur*. Rather than threatening a legal battle, Becker demonstrated his remarkable adroitness by ringing Signoret to say that he understood, and that he could easily replace her: 'So, the next day, I took the train to Paris. I went back, and just as well I did: I went back to make perhaps the most beautiful film of my life.'[35]

Becker also maintained some level of continuity in the members of the crew he employed. Foremost among his collaborators was Marguerite Houllé-Renoir, who edited all of his films but one (*Les Aventures d'Arsène Lupin*, edited by her niece, Geneviève Vaury), and who had previously worked and lived with Jean Renoir.[36] It is thanks to her skill as an editor that Becker's films retain their flowing tempo, in spite of the extraordinary number of edits that they contained. As Houllé-Renoir herself puts it, the large number of joins in the film is not noticed because 'it matched in terms of feeling'.[37] The director of photography, Robert Lefebvre, had already worked on *Edouard et Caroline*, which was shot on a low budget and a very tight schedule. In a letter to one financial backer, Becker cited Lefebvre's professionalism and efficiency as an important contribution to ensuring that *Casque d'or* would be completed on time.[38] Many of those involved on the technical side were associated with the quality tradition: Lefebvre thanks to his work with Claude Autant-Lara, René Clair, Henri Decoin and Christian-Jaque; Jean d'Eaubonne through his work for Max Ophüls; and Georges Van Parys through his music for René Clair. The producers certainly used this in their bid for a government advance, citing the participation of Lefebvre, d'Eaubonne, Signoret and Becker as evidence of the film's 'importance'. They were successful in obtaining a loan of FF 18 million (less than the FF 30 million requested).[39]

Given *Casque d'or*'s renunciation of the costume drama frills, Jean d'Eaubonne – established as a set designer since the 1930s and best known for his rather 'baroque' sets for *La Ronde* (1950) and *Le Plaisir* (1952) – initially seems an odd choice for production designer. D'Eaubonne's main responsibilities were the design of the sets for the Ange Gabriel, and the street, hotel and prison courtyard of the execution sequence. The Ange Gabriel, along with Leca's house, can be seen as belonging to this extremely elaborate style of décor with a strong emphasis on screens, windows, mirrors and other highly polished surfaces – all of which emphasise Leca's vanity and duplicity, and contrast with the simplicity of other décors and especially the real locations. The costumes, designed by Antoine Mayo, also function to develop character. Mayo was principally a painter, and only worked on a few films, notably those of Marcel Carné. His first film designs were for *Les Enfants du paradis*, as a favour for Jacques Prévert, another film that challenges the traditional costume drama through its emphasis on realism and its popular cultural references.[40] Mayo's contribution to *Casque d'or* has been summarised by Andrew as having created 'understated costumes' that are 'worn not strutted', contributing greatly to the authenticity of the film.[41]

Music does not just feature for 'atmosphere' in Becker's films, but also plays an important diegetic role,[42] and this is also true in *Casque d'or*. Georges Van Parys, who composed the original music for *Casque d'or*, had been celebrated as a composer since the 1930s, having worked on films such as *L'Age d'or* (Buñuel, 1930), *Le Million/The Million* (René Clair, 1931) *Zouzou* (Marc Allégret, 1934) and *Un mauvais garçon/Counsel for Romance* (Jean Boyer, 1936), and he remained one of the best-known film composers throughout the 1950s, for example with his music for *French Cancan* (Renoir, 1954). In *Casque d'or*, his music ranges from the diegetic (the dance tunes, the wedding music, as well as the less conventional birdsong) to the non-diegetic (Leca's jaunty theme), and also blends with Clément's haunting song *Le Temps des cerises* that dominates the end of the film.

Casque d'or, as we have seen, was made in the professional realm of the tradition of quality. And yet, as Dudley Andrew has pointed out, the film has acquired a legend that inscribes it within an artisanal, communitarian vision of film-making characterised by teamwork, honesty and authenticity.[43] This means that ethically as well as aesthetically, *Casque d'or* is situated simultaneously within and outside of the dominant cinema, as Truffaut noted.[44] Let us now turn to an examination of French films of the time, in order to see how *Casque d'or* relates to its cinematic context.

Casque d'or and French cinema

One important legacy of Truffaut's 1954 battle-cry 'A certain tendency of French cinema', is that the mainstream cinema of this decade – the tradition of quality, or the '*cinéma de papa*', has tended to be dismissed as unworthy of study: as over-literary, uncinematic and unrepresentative. While these criticisms are undoubtedly well founded in many cases, the enormous popularity of French cinema during the 1950s, the final decade of its dominance as a form of visual entertainment, suggests that Truffaut does not tell the whole story, deliberately playing down many remarkable films such as *Manèges* (Yves Allégret, 1950), *La Vérité sur Bébé Donge* (Decoin, 1952) or *Le Diable au corps* (Autant-Lara, 1947) in order to make his polemical point. (Truffaut would soon adopt a more moderate position towards the mainstream cinema.)[45] This is also a time of important technical developments in French cinema, many of which benefited New Wave directors (lighter cameras, faster film stock, but also cinemascope and more widespread use of colour), and there is an increasing emphasis on the spectacular as a way of rivalling Hollywood imports. The development of popular genres is also an important aspect that can be seen to go beyond the 'straightforward' crime thriller and the literary adaptation that are often seen as dominating the period, along with that other domestic staple, comedy.[46] Recent work on this decade and studies of popular French cinema have demonstrated that there is more to this decade's cinema than critical fashion may have dictated and that, instead of subscribing to New Wave 'myths of rebellion', there are good reasons to look for points of continuity across classical and so-called New Wave cinemas.[47] It has already been suggested that *Casque d'or* offers one of these points, sitting uneasily within the dominant tradition of quality. We will now go on to examine the reasons for this, looking at some examples of quality-tradition films as points of comparison. However, we will first turn to an examination of *Casque d'or* in relation to the 1930s cinema to which it has often been compared. Dudley Andrew has identified *Casque d'or* as a film bathed in the left-wing nostalgia for this decade, but does this necessarily preclude it from having any contemporary relevance, as some critics argued?[48]

Cinematic antecedents

Dudley Andrew argues that the solid artisanship of *Casque d'or* returns us to Renoir's 'vision of film-making' thanks to the portrayal of Manda's professional skill, the carefully crafted nature of the film and direct references to Renoir's

Une Partie de campagne (1936, released in 1946). Becker was first assistant on this film, and was involved in preparing the film for public release ten years later.[49] *Une Partie de campagne* closes where *Casque d'or* opens, on the river, with the heroine rowing her snivelling partner while he complains. The Parisian custom of visiting the countryside on holidays (to eat and drink and to go fishing) is evoked in both films, and, linked to this, the two films make the association between proximity to nature and heightened sensuality. The earlier film shows Madame Dufour (Jane Marken) – corset undone – tickling her husband's ear with a blade of grass – an action repeated by Marie – while her daughter, Henriette (Sylvia Bataille), is strangely disturbed by her surroundings. Both heroines excite the emotions and jealousies of the men around them, but unlike Marie, Henriette is innocent of the effect of her actions upon the men around her. They are both aware of desire, but in Henriette's case it remains untargeted, and she remains unable to speak about her desire other than in the vaguest terms – contrasting strongly with Marie, who knows exactly what she wants: 'I wanted to come, so I took a cab,' she says to Manda. In this respect, Marie is more like the heroine of what Andrew terms the swansong of Poetic Realism, *Les Enfants du paradis*. Garance (Arletty), like Marie, is full of Parisian *gouaille* (bold repartee) and views the world (and men) through an ironic eye – and she also declares to Baptiste that love is simple. Both Garance and Marie accept an offer to become the possession of a man, but while Marie immediately regrets her decision (she shudders as Leca brushes her bare shoulder with his hand) and spends the rest of the film fighting against her situation, Garance suffers in silence, returning night after night to the Funambules Theatre to see what could have been been, but only confronting Baptiste when her identity is discovered.

Andrew asserts that *Casque d'or*, as a project that pre-dates the war, 'comes through the Occupation and Liberation preserving the poetic realist sensibility' and he finds much in common between the taciturn Manda and the mime, Baptiste (Jean-Louis Barrault).[50] However, I would argue that there is a major difference between these two characters, and that this is the difference between the hangover of pre-war fatalism and a post-war Existentialist sensibility. When Garance (Arletty) offers herself freely to Baptiste, he refuses her because he wishes to preserve the image of idealised femininity that she embodies for him. Manda, on the other hand, must fight for Marie, but when he has won her he takes her for what she is with no illusions. For both Manda and Marie act according to their desires but also their responsibilities – this is what gives these characters their integrity. They also know they must make the most of whatever time they have. Baptiste's mimes expressing his alienation take place on stage – they are mere representations – whereas Manda's forthright actions are rooted in the 'real' world. Becker's characters belong in the post-war period and make their own destiny: his film may end in tragedy but it has nothing to do with the fatalism that stalked the doomed heroes of this pre-war cinema.[51]

So, if *Casque d'or* draws on these 1930s classics, it can be said to do so in a knowingly referential way. While these citations may not be as direct or as numerous as in many of the New Wave films, they do reveal the cinephilia of Becker and others involved in the film, a passion shared with the younger generation of film-makers. Another example of this playful referencing is in the name of the corrupt policeman, Inspector Juliani – a final reconciliation with Renoir over *Le Crime de Monsieur Lange*, where a certain Inspector Giuliani, Batala's cousin, turns up to profit from his 'death'? And Becker's film does not only draw on 1930s French classics. Georges Sadoul picked up on the film's debt to Feuillade's crime series, such as *Fantômas* (1913–1914) and *Les Vampires* (1915–1916), which provided Becker with images of the apparatus of the law, from the caped policemen to the vehicles and the prison courtyard where the execution takes place.[52] *Fantômas à l'ombre de la guillotine*, for example, recounts a daring escape by the master criminal, involving a hotel room very similar to the one from which Marie watches Manda's execution, as well as other details such as the prisoner's white shirt with the collar removed. *Casque d'or* shows a similarly eager crowd assembled for the execution: people are craning their necks in order to see Manda's receive the blade. Becker's film, with its sparse dialogue, can be seen in many ways to replicate these silent films that he admired so much. For example, Manda and Raymond's escape, running the length of the street and leaping onto the moving carriage that brought Marie, while she throws herself at the pursuing policeman, could be taken straight from an episode of *Les Vampires*, although Becker's film uses the sounds of gunshots, running footsteps and galloping hooves to convey the panic of the moment. Of course, Feuillade's filming technique achieved a 'reality effect' of showing the Paris streets as they were without need of reconstruction.[53] This was an effect Becker worked hard to replicate in earlier films, from *Boudu sauvé des eaux* (Renoir, 1932) to *Rendez-vous de juillet*, but in *Casque d'or* he needed to reconstruct the period – complete with shoppers on the streets, customers and advertisements at the *guinguette*, the Ange Gabriel and Danard's workshop, for example. In this way, *Casque d'or* can be seen to tread a very careful line between realism and stylisation. As Andrew argues, Becker's film only increases its aura of authenticity by drawing on cinematic history in order to tell his tale of the turn-of-the-century *apaches* (gangsters), thus presenting a nostalgic layering of historical and cinematic moments.[54] It does so fondly and knowingly, prefiguring the early films of Truffaut (*Tirez sur le pianiste* and *Jules et Jim* would in turn pay homage to *Casque d'or*) and Godard. And this fascination with the past does not prevent this tale of love, friendship, resistance, treachery and denunciation from also being firmly rooted in its own time.

Casque d'or *and its contemporaries*

Mainstream French cinema of the 1950s was marked by a striving for technical perfection, earning it the 'quality' label, as we have seen. However, it was also characterised by what Susan Hayward has termed 'voluntarist myopia' relating to the issues of the time and of the recent past, continuing the Occupation cinema trends of escapist melodramas and comedies.[55] Though French cinema had faced a crisis in the immediate post-war years when faced with Hollywood competition, it began to recover in the late 1940s thanks to the reform of the Blum-Byrnes agreements and the introduction of government subsidies. By the 1950s, cinema had recovered to become France's second most important industry after car manufacturing.[56]

The need to compete with Hollywood films for spectators led also to an increase in co-productions (especially with Italy and Spain), which permitted larger budgets, and therefore more spectacular pictures. Homegrown stars such as Jean Marais, Gérard Philipe, Michèle Morgan and Martine Carol, and later, of course, Brigitte Bardot, were also pitted against the Americans. Popular genres – comedy, thrillers and costume films in particular – came to reflect the national context, often through the adaptation of literary works.

So where does *Casque d'or* fit into this cinema? A medium-budget film, it did not require the level of financing of a co-production, but, as we have seen, its producers called upon the experience and talent of those involved in its creation to win a substantial subsidy in the form of a low-interest loan. As a costume film, it also corresponds generically to the trends of mainstream cinema. And yet, *Casque d'or* also stands apart from the dominant cinema of the 1950s for several reasons. Most obviously, it shuns the literary style that Truffaut so decried, paring down the dialogue to its bare minimum. Manda is a man of actions not words, who can be seen as embodying a new kind of masculinity that would be explored further in films from *Touchez pas au grisbi* to *Le Samouraï* (Melville, 1967). Indeed, Melville cast Reggiani as Faugel in *Le Doulos* (1962) because he saw the character as 'Manda's grandson'.[57] Neither is *Casque d'or* adapted from a literary source. While French production of this time (from costume dramas to crime films) tended to be dominated by literary adaptations, Becker's film shows fidelity to its visual sources (*Le Petit illustré*, the paintings of Renoir) but entirely rewrites the narrative of the *fait divers* on which it is based.

Casque d'or is a costume film but not one that falls into the dominant patterns of this genre as it was most often seen in 1950s French cinema. It draws heavily on the iconography of the gangster film for its backdrop – indeed, the *milieu* features as more than just décor since it is from this environment that Manda and Marie are desperate to escape. But the film also draws on the iconography of other genres: its melodramatic storyline, and the silent stoicism of its hero, are reminiscent of the Western – with Belleville featuring here as the lawless frontier town (it was, of course, a *quartier de barrière* – one of the outlying districts of Paris that formed a band around the more salubrious areas of the city) filled with prostitutes and outlaws known as *apaches* – and the Ange Gabriel as the 'saloon' where the deadly duel takes place. Even the costumes can be said to approximate Western garb: in particular the hats worn by the *apaches*, the ties Manda and Danard wear in a bow, and the kerchief Manda wears knotted around his neck.

Casque d'or, then, draws on more than one genre, but it is arguably by its realism that it stands out most from the more usual forms of costume drama of the time: comic escapism, lavishly sophisticated literary adaptations and melodrama. By focusing on the banal details of everyday life, not just of the main protagonists but also of the secondary characters, who are always seen engaged in some routine activity, Becker paints an intimate portrait of this world. *Casque d'or* is a melodrama that is inscribed in the realist cinematic tradition by the minimalism of its *mise-en-scène*, of its dialogues and of the actors' performances, all of which emphasise the 'authentic'. Stylistically, then, it is quite different from successful quality productions such as *Caroline chérie* (Pottier, 1950) or *Fanfan la tulipe* (Christian-Jaque, 1952).

Caroline chérie, a vehicle for France's most popular female star of the time, Martine Carol, uses the pretext of historical reconstruction to offer the spectacle of Carol's alluringly compliant body.[58] The use of an ironic male voiceover distances the spectator from the characters, privileging spectacle over narrative. *Fanfan la tulipe*, while celebrating the courage and ingenuity of the people and satirising the aristocracy as well as the futility of war, also foregrounds spectacle: once again of the historical reconstruction (castles, barracks, convents and eighteenth-century rural idylls) and of the stars, Gérard Philipe as Fanfan and Gina Lollobrigida as Adeline. Both stars are offered for erotic contemplation: a bare-chested Philipe pontificates on love while washing himself, while Lollobrigida's gypsy-look costumes, with plunging necklines and tightly laced corsets, draw attention to the barely concealed body beneath.

This kind of swashbuckling epic was not the only kind of historical film to enjoy popularity at this time. A remarkable number of films were set in the Belle Epoque: fifty between 1945 and 1959.[59] According to Susan Hayward, this attests to the escapism of post-war cinema, while Geneviève Sellier sees many of these films as addressing issues of gender relations in a more daring way than many films with contemporary settings.[60] Two films that could be said to represent the range of Belle Epoque pictures are *Gigi* (Jacqueline Audry, 1948) and *La Ronde* (Max Ophüls, 1950). Based on literary sources (Colette and Arthur Schnitzler), both are sophisticated comedies of manners, which deal with the sexual double standard, yet, while in *Gigi* 'true love' prevails over the cynical exchange system of the *demi-monde*, *La Ronde* shows that all relations between the sexes are manipulative and that the double standard triumphs most strongly in marriage. Both these films emphasise the frills of the Belle Epoque as emblematic of the superficiality of society – a theme picked up by *Casque d'or* in relation to Leca. In *La Ronde*, Signoret once again plays a prostitute, but nothing like Marie. Her nameless pliancy deprives her of agency, while the soft-focus close-ups of her face framed by the feather boa that connotes her profession reduce her to the stereotypical whore.

What all these films have in common, and where *Casque d'or* differs, is that, while Becker's film strives for authenticity and realism, they all undermine realism from the outset. For example, in *Fanfan* the spectator is addressed directly by the King/narrator, whose telescopic view stands in for ours, while in *La Ronde* the narrator shows us round the set, and interrupts the film to address the viewer.

In its rejection of such distancing devices that call attention to the cinematic form, then, *Casque d'or* is perhaps closer to the strand of realist melodramas of 1950s French costume cinema: films such as *Gervaise* (Clément, 1956), which demonstrates the same meticulous concern with re-creating its period – in this case achieved by filming in studios on extensive and elaborate sets designed by Paul Bertrand. *Gervaise* is based on Zola's *L'Assommoir*, and follows the attempts of its heroine (played by Maria Schell) to make good in spite of her alcoholic husband, Coupeau (François Périer), her good-for-nothing former lover, Lantier (Armand Mestral), and the plottings of the jealous Virginie. She manages to open her own shop, but Coupeau drinks the profits, and eventually smashes it up, leaving Gervaise and her youngest daughter, Nana, destitute. At the end, Gervaise has also turned to alcohol.

Yet, though both films are realist melodramas, there are also significant differences in their approaches. Adapted from its literary source by Jean Aurenche and Pierre Bost, *Gervaise* follows in the literary cinematic tradition, while *Casque d'or* is much less reliant on words. In *Gervaise*, the eponymous heroine introduces the film with a voiceover that recurs with every major ellipsis, orientating the spectator – a device much more necessary when the narrative takes place over many years. This difference in scale between the two films is also a visual one: Clément's film features impressive set pieces, such as the fight at the wash-house between Gervaise and Virginie, Gervaise's birthday party and the courtroom scene, while *Casque d'or* is a much more intimate film, creating an impression of a *milieu* in a much more economical way. Even the sequences set at the *guinguette* and the Ange Gabriel are on a much smaller scale, with fewer extras and smaller sets. Correspondingly, *Gervaise* contains a good number of extremely long shots to show off the remarkable sets of these poor areas of Paris, whereas *Casque d'or* favours the medium long shot that privileges the actors. Both films are concerned with re-creating a certain community: the difference is that, while Clément meticulously portrays this in all its material detail, Becker looks for it in the characters, in their gestures and in their interactions with each other. Likewise, both films feature the unsuccessful struggles of their female protagonists to escape from an oppressive condition: that of lowly employee and wife of an alcoholic in the case of Gervaise, and for Marie, that of prostitute. It is to this question of the depiction of women in French cinema that we now turn.

Fourth Republic cinema and gender relations: a crisis in femininity

> Only … Becker can say, like Napoléon, my women are my victories. His films follow a logical series of female portraits endowed with real psychological, social and romantic meaning … [61]

Casque d'or is a remarkable film for its time in terms of its representation of gender relations, with an actively desiring heroine and a central couple who are equal within their relationship – far from commonplace within French cinema of the time. The late 1940s and early 1950s witnessed a shift in gender representation from Occupation cinema that corresponded with the rather difficult post-war renegotiation of gender roles. Although this was not a time marked by any concerted feminist movement, 1944 saw women's acquisition of the right to vote, the Constitution of the Fourth Republic, ratified in 1946, finally recognised women as equal to men, and in 1949, Simone de Beauvoir published *The Second Sex*, which immediately became a bestseller.[62] At the same time, though, women were being persuaded by government initiatives, the mainstream and women's press and at school or at church that their role was to stand aside and let the men take over once more; that their duty lay in the domestic sphere and especially in motherhood, since France was in desperate need of repopulation: de Gaulle famously called for 12 million bouncing babies. The return of 1.2 million prisoners of war, 700,000 conscripts who had been sent to work in Germany under compulsory work schemes (the Service de Travail Obligatoire, STO, introduced in February 1943) and 400,000 deportees returning from concentration camps and other places was often far from straightforward, and many relationships did not survive the years of separation.[63] During the war, women had assumed responsibilities traditionally seen as the province of men, in addition to their usual tasks made more onerous by the Occupation conditions. Thus, for many, the Liberation brought a considerable lightening of their burden as tasks were shared out once again. However, they were not necessarily content to return to the traditional division of labour.

There was also a distinct suspicion surrounding women's sexuality at this time: one of the most shockingly violent and shameful aspects of the Liberation purges was the public shearing of women accused of 'horizontal collaboration' and the parading of these women – known as *les femmes tondues* – through the streets and the village squares. Many have argued that the spectacular and often extremely violent nature of these summary reprisals suggests that they were not just a punishment for past acts, but also acted as a warning to all women as to the consequences of failing to toe the patriarchal line.[64] Purges were also carried out with the film industry and although men were punished for ideological or professional collaboration (notably Clouzot, Pierre Fresnay and Maurice Chevalier), women were accused of sexual collaboration and punished equally severely (though none of them was shorn): Arletty and Mireille Balin were imprisoned at the time of the Liberation, while Ginette Leclerc paid for her French lover's crimes with a year in prison.[65] Of these women, only Arletty managed – up to a point – to revive her career after the war.

Given this context, then, it is perhaps unsurprising that a particular obsession with gender relations can be discerned in the cinema of this time – albeit one that most critics deem unworthy of comment. This section will offer an overview of the dominant cinematic trends in this area. While the political and social agenda is to reinforce traditional gender boundaries, and put forward 'positive' images of masculinity and femininity, cinema, it seems, is frequently more concerned with the less avowable fears and desires – psychological wounds opened up by the war and the Occupation – revealing a crisis in femininity at this time of reconstruction of gender roles.

One exception to the general critical silence on this issue is an article by Doniol-Valcroze, published in the *Cahiers du cinéma* in 1954, which focuses on the representation of women in Fourth Republic French cinema, and decries the emergence of a new female figure: the *femme-objet*.[66] Though Doniol-Valcroze can hardly be aligned with feminism (in his article the spectator is consistently constructed as male, and female attitudes towards these representations are not considered at all), he is nonetheless almost alone in commenting on these trends, and his argument is therefore a useful starting point for any discussion of cinematic gender relations at this time.

Doniol-Valcroze details the roles and narrative functions of female characters and who played them in the most successful films since 1945. Out of over 800 French films, only 60 are deemed to contain 'one or several heroines worthy of the name, that's to say with real depth' – the rest fall into stereotypical categories such as 'garce' or prostitute.[67] In addition to this increasingly stereotyped representation, Doniol-Valcroze notes that the *femme-objet* also denotes an increasing eroticisation of femininity, since typically, these women are put in situations where they must deploy their only weapon – their sexuality – to defend themselves. And to push his analysis further, this inevitably means that these women must also be contained at the end of the film, either brought back into patriarchal line within a heterosexual relationship, or punished for their misdemeanours. The huge success of Martine Carol in *Caroline chérie* (Richard Pottier, 1950), her breakthrough role, or *Nana* (Christian-Jaque, 1954), in which her sexuality was exploited to the full and offered for the contemplation of the (male) spectator in a docile and unchallenging form, highlights the box office potential of the erotic *femme-objet* at this time – a potential that would be exploited even further by the young Brigitte Bardot and her generation (including Cécile Aubry, Françoise Arnoul and Dany Carrel).

Burch and Sellier, in their ground-breaking work on gender relations in French cinema from 1930 to 1956, have identified major trends in the depiction of masculinity and femininity at this time.[68] They argue that gender representation is the ground on to which the pathologies of the war years (defeat, Occupation, collaboration, humiliation) – pathologies not directly addressed in Fourth Republic cinema – have been displaced. As a result, just as the *femmes tondues* became the public scapegoats for the nation's shame, so French cinema at this time also can be said to equate the female body with the nation, and, therefore, to construct female sexuality as something potentially dangerous that must be controlled by men. Thus it is not the patriotic figure of Marianne, the embodiment of the Republic, who comes to dominate female representation at this time. Rather it is the 'garce' or bitch, eclipsed in the cinema of the Occupation, who makes a resounding comeback in Fourth Republic cinema – especially in films belonging to the post-war vein of *réalisme noir* (black realism) – wreaking havoc on her innocent male victims by her ambition, sexual appetite and greed. Films such as *Panique* (Duvivier, 1946), *Le Diable au corps* (Autant-Lara, 1947), *Manon* (Clouzot, 1948), *Manèges* (Yves Allégret, 1950) and *Voici le temps des assassins* (Duvivier, 1956) feature stars such as Viviane Romance, Micheline Presle, Cécile Aubry, Simone Signoret and Danièle Delorme in roles where they cause the downfall of one or more men, either deliberately, or (even more insidiously) unwittingly, simply because they cannot help their destructive nature. The punishments meted out to these women are often so severe that they could be seen to serve as a warning to others, and to reflect a general fear of femininity.

Just as the head-shavings can also be seen as a warning to all women not to step out of line, so the misogyny that can be identified in many Fourth Republic films also relates to the contemporary crisis in femininity: to women's increasing role in the public sphere (of work and politics) and the paradoxical number of measures designed to ensure that women remain firmly within the domestic sphere, including the single-wage benefit, generous allowances for large families and the fact that husbands could still prevent their wives from working until 1965.[69]

Burch and Sellier's work offers a nuanced reading of gender representations, which takes into consideration industrial and economic factors such as increasing competition with Hollywood, the rise of the big-budget European co-production and the increasing codification of genres during the late 1940s and 1950s. In particular, shifting popularity in genres since the Occupation can be seen to foreground certain gender identities. The return of the *polar*, or detective thriller, places the male protagonist (cop or gangster) firmly at the centre. While these films offer quite different images of masculinity – from the ultra-confident, macho violence and sexuality played out in exotic locations of the Lemmy Caution films, to the more homespun, quieter and more vulnerable (though still dangerous and sexually attractive) heroes of *Grisbi*, or *Du Rififi chez les hommes* (Dassin, 1955) – the images of women are very similar in both types of *polar*. In the Lemmy Caution films, women are blonde, voluptuous and interchangeable: the forerunner of the Bond girl, their 'dangerous' sexuality is easily tamed or eliminated by the hero. In what we might call the French 'heist' movies, older women feature marginally as 'maternal' figures, running prostitutes, nightclubs or restaurants, whereas younger women – also peripheral to the narrative – are engaged in euphemistic 'professions' that maximise their spectacular potential: dancers, singers, waitresses and striptease artists. (*Rififi*'s representation of the young family makes it something of an exception.) These women are all defined solely by their sexuality, which will either be 'tamed' as they fall for the hero, like Carlotta de la Rue (Dominique Wilms) in *La Môme Vert-de-gris* – a singer whose name suggests another profession – or will prove treacherous, like Josy (Jeanne Moreau) in *Grisbi*, or Anne in *Bob le flambeur*, both of whom betray the secrets of their men to their rivals with whom they are also sleeping.[70] Even more extreme is the representation of women in the emerging genre that became known as *réalisme noir*, epitomised by Yves Allégret's trilogy *Dédée d'Anvers* (1947), *Une si jolie petite plage* (1948) and *Manèges* (1950). These films offer viciously misogynistic representations of exploitative women while men are reduced to little more than the victims of these scheming harpies. These women are often severely punished: in *Manèges* the mother/ daughter team, out to fleece Bernard Blier for all they can, get their come-uppance when Dora, the daughter, is paralysed in a car accident. On the other hand, the continued popularity of the costume drama, considered a more 'feminine' genre, could be seen as an opportunity for more 'positive' images of women. However, a large number of these films, as we have seen above, in fact present nothing more than the *femme-objet* identified by Doniol-Valcroze: the erotic female body placed at the service of patriarchy.

Masculinity in these films (often handsomely embodied by the 'soft and gentle' Gérard Philipe)[71] is frequently romantic and idealistic, with the hero's fantasies defining the feminine ideal (in *Fanfan* Philipe's character believes Adeline's false prophecy that he will marry the King's daughter, and in *Belles de nuit* he plays a young music teacher who daydreams of alternative existences as a great lover in various different historical periods). These films reinforce traditional gender stereotypes, presenting men as active and women as passive yet devious. Most of all – and this is far from neutral in a post-war climate, which is also marked by wars of decolonisation in Indochina and in Algeria from 1954 – women remain defined by their sexuality even, and perhaps especially, in the face of momentous political upheaval. Caroline makes her way through revolutionary France saving her skin (and her head) thanks to her easy virtue. And however satirical *Fanfan la tulipe*'s attitude to war may be, the film equates national pride, military victory and female virginity. The country may be at war, but Adeline's resistance (albeit to her own King) is purely sexual. Her desirable virginity distils an ideal of French womanhood (embodied by an Italian!) which is diametrically opposed to that spectacularised by the *femmes tondues* at the Liberation, but which can still only envisage femininity in terms of women's sexuality.

Fortunately, this somewhat depressing account does not tell the whole story. Geneviève Sellier has pointed out that within the genre of the costume film there is a group of films that can be said to offer a more radical view of gender roles by foregrounding patriarchal inequalities.[72] These films, including *Casque d'or* as well as *Occupe toi d'Amélie* (Autant-Lara, 1949), *Madame de* (Ophüls, 1953), *Gigi* (Audry, 1949) and *French Cancan* (Renoir, 1954), are set in the Belle Epoque, and, according to Sellier, offer a female perspective on the oppressive patriarchal structures of heterosexuality. Sellier has identified at least 50 of these films made between 1945 and 1959, including at least one film by most of the major directors of the time, including Autant-Lara, Becker, Clouzot, Ophüls, Clair, Renoir and Daquin, and featuring most of the output of the only female director working in mainstream French cinema at this time, Jacqueline Audry. We might also include *Gervaise* in this group, even though it is set well before the Belle Epoque, thanks to its complex portrayal of a passionate, vengeful, sexual woman – a mother and wife who also has ambitions for herself – even if they end in the bottle. And, if we further extend Sellier's analysis to look at stars, it is notable that, though many of the male stars are the same as in the swashbuckling erotic historical film outlined above (e.g. Gérard Philipe, Jean Desailly and Jean Marais), the Belle Epoque films tend to be associated with different female stars: Danielle Darrieux, Michèle Morgan and Danièle Delorme in particular, but also Simone Signoret. Though these stars clearly have an erotic appeal, they are not solely defined by their sexuality; indeed, they are often associated with a more cerebral or 'intelligent' performance style, and of course, unlike Carol and Bardot, none of them appeared nude.[73]

Arguably, even within this genre, *Casque d'or* stands out thanks to its condemnation of patriarchal structures. While other films foreground female oppression and give a prominence to female protagonists absent from other genres, they are often ultimately supportive of the status quo. *French Cancan*, for example, sees nothing strange in the couple formed by Gabin and Françoise Arnoul in spite of their age difference, and indeed characterises her jealousy as placing an unfair demand on the male genius – and his former mistress and her mother persuade her that she is being unreasonable![74]

As in *Le Carrosse d'or* (1952), in *French Cancan* Renoir offers a highly constructed colour spectacle, using colour, elaborate choreography and studio shooting to foreground the role of art. The film pays homage to *Casque d'or* in its opening scene, when two young ruffians comment on the presence of the wealthy crowd of thrill-seekers in the notorious nightclub where Danglard (Gabin) will meet Nini (Arnoul), and also features Pâquerette as an ancient former dancer fallen on hard times. The extravagant finale of the Cancan performance at the opening night of the Moulin Rouge is only made possible by Nini's acceptance of the transfer of Danglard's affections to his new 'recruit'. Like Becker's *Falbalas*, this film presents creative genius as dependent on sexual conquests, but, unlike *Falbalas*, sees nothing problematic about this, and presents the members of the 'harem' as slightly hysterical but ultimately accepting of the situation.

The costume film is not the only genre to address gender issues, however. Some exceptional films with contemporary settings also place gender relations at their heart, including melodramas such as *La Vérité sur Bébé Donge* (Henri Decoin, 1952), in which the female viewpoint is privileged, and Bébé's actions 'absolved' by the understanding investigating judge, and the spectator who witnesses the constant humiliation of a woman trapped in marriage because of her financial dependence on her husband. Becker's domestic comedies, *Antoine et Antoinette* and *Edouard et Caroline*, show the female partners as more dynamic than their husbands, who suffer from a sense of (sexual) insecurity. The critical responses to these films (weak plotlines, failing to address working conditions) reveal just how low gender issues featured on the agenda of most 1950s cinema critics. This is also shown by the refusal to distribute Grémillon's remarkable 'feminist' film *L'Amour d'une femme* (1954), featuring Micheline Presle as a doctor forced to choose between romantic love and her profession. She chooses medicine, but the fact that she is faced with such a dilemma reflects the situation of many French women at this time.[75]

Within this context, then, we can see that Marie and Manda's relationship of equal partners in *Casque d'or* is remarkable, and is an important reason why the film did not sit easily with the orthodoxies of its time. We can begin to see, then, just how different *Casque d'or* was from most of its contemporaries, using its past setting to address some extremely contemporary issues that were largely disavowed or ignored in mainstream cinema.

Casque d'or, then, treads a line between the norm and the exception, in many ways. In terms of Becker's films, it reveals his concern with the portrayal of authentic characters and their environment, as well as the major recurring themes in his work of the relations between men and women, masculine friendship and loyalty and betrayal. However, it is the first of his films to step outside a contemporary setting. In terms of the cinema of its time, it falls within a popular genre (the Belle Epoque film), using well-known stars and actors, and utilising the technical expertise of the 'quality tradition', yet it deliberately plays down the spectacular aspects of the period film, preferring a working-class setting drawn from popular culture over the more usual lavish literary adaptations that focus on the bourgeoisie, and emphasising authenticity rather than the artifice often associated with the costume film. We shall now turn to a discussion of the form and style of the film, in order to examine this in more detail.

Notes

1 Naumann, Claude, *Jacques Becker: Entre classicisme et modernité* (Paris: BIFI/Durante, 2001), p. 13.
2 Prédal, René, *Le Cinéma français depuis 1945* (Paris: Nathan, 1991), p. 54. Becker did not work on *Toni* because he was busy making a short film of his own with Pierre Prévert, *Le Commissaire est bon enfant*, or on *Le Crime de Monsieur Lange* because of a quarrel (outlined below).
3 See Naumann: *Jacques Becker*, p. 23, and Naumann, Claude, 'La Réception critique des films de Jacques Becker: première partie, de *Dernier atout à Casque d'or*, 22 November 2002, http://www.proto.bifi.fr/cineregards/article.asp?rub=1. Accessed 8 August 2005.
4 Journalist, writer and politician. Editor of *Elle*, co-founder of *L'Express* in 1953, and Secretary of State for Women's Affairs, and then for Culture (1974–1977). Giroud (1916–2003) was noted especially as a commentator on the position of women in French society.
5 Cited in Naumann: *Jacques Becker*, p. 177.
6 Chevalier, Louis, *Montmartre du plaisir et du crime* (Paris: Robert Laffont, 1980), p. 281.
7 Interview with Georges Sadoul in *Les Lettres françaises*, April 1952, cited in Vignaux, Valérie, *Jacques Becker ou l'exercice de la liberté* (Liège: Editions du Céfal, 2001), p. 127.
8 Lanoux, Armand, 'La Vraie Casque d'or', in Gilbert Guilleminault (ed.), *Le Roman vrai de la Troisième République: La Belle Epoque* (Paris: Denoël, 1958), p. 117.
9 Varennes, Henri de, 'Gazette des Tribunaux. Cour d'assises de la Seine: Casque d'or', *Le Figaro*, 31 May 1902, pp. 3–4.
10 See Lanoux: 'La Vraie Casque d'or', pp. 72, 76 and 99.
11 Corbin, Alain, *Women for Hire: Prostitution and sexuality in France after 1850*, trans. by Alan Sheridan (Cambridge, MA and London: Harvard University Press, 1990), p. viii.
12 Hélie, Amélie, 'Mémoires ou histoire de Casque d'or racontée par elle-même, ou Ma Vie pas Casque d'or', *Fin de siècle*, 5 June 1902, p. 1.
13 Corbin: *Women for Hire*, pp. 200–201.
14 Lanoux: 'La Vraie Casque d'or', passim.
15 See Lanoux: 'La Vraie Casque d'or', pp. 81–88.
16 Lanoux: 'La Vraie Casque d'or', p. 84.
17 The Bonnot gang – a group of extremist anarchists known as illegalists – sowed mayhem and murder in France and Belgium from 1910 until their capture in spectacular seiges and shoot-outs in April 1912, which attracted thousands of onlookers. A film was made about their exploits, *La Bande à Bonnot* (Fourastié, 1969), starring Bruno Crémer, Jacques Brel and Annie Girardot. See also Guilleminault: *Le Roman vrai de la Troisième République* vol. 4 pp. 151–216, and *La Bande à Bonnot*, http://www.chez.com/durru/bonnot/bande.htm. Accessed 7 June 2005.
18 Interview with Sadoul, cited in Vignaux: *Jacques Becker*, p. 127.
19 See Sagner-Düchting, Karin, *Renoir: Paris and the Belle Epoque* (Munich and New York: Prestel, 1996).
20 Andrew, Dudley, '*Casque d'or, casquettes*, a cask of aging wine: Jacques Becker's *Casque d'or* (1952)', in Susan Hayward and Ginette Vincendeau (eds), *French*

Film: Texts and Contexts (London and New York: Routledge, 2000), p. 124, fn. 1; and Sagner-Düchting: *Renoir: Paris and the Belle Epoque*, p. 54.

21   *A la Villette*, Aristide Bruant, trans. by Raymond Rudorff. Rudorff, Raymond, *Belle Epoque: Paris in the Nineties* (London: Hamish Hamilton, 1972), pp. 80–81.

22   Rudorff: *Belle Epoque*, p. 75.

23   Bellanger, Claude, Jacques Godechot, Pierre Guiral and Fernand Terrou (eds), *Histoire générale de la presse française: Vol. 3 1871–1940* (5 vols.) (Paris: Presses Universitaires de France, 1972), p. 390.

24   Andrew: '*Casque d'or, casquettes*', p. 123.

25   Signoret, Simone, *La Nostalgie n'est plus ce qu'elle était* (Paris: Seuil, 1978), p. 115.

26   Hayward, Susan, *Simone Signoret: The Star as Cultural Sign* (London and New York: Continuum, 2004), p. 98.

27   Rivette, Jacques and François Truffaut, 'Entretien avec Jacques Becker', *Cahiers du cinéma* 32 (February 1954), pp. 3–17, p. 12. See also Vignaux: *Jacques Becker*, pp. 124–127, for an account of the dispute with Duvivier.

28   The production archive shows that Antoine, who wrote the script for *Quai des brumes* (Carné, 1938), held the script rights to *Casque d'or* in 1951. This is held at the BiFi, 51 Rue de Bercy, 75012 Paris.

29   These details are taken from the script held in the BiFi archive and from Vignaux: *Jacques Becker*, p. 124. In an interview, Becker refers to this character as Deibler (Rivette and Truffaut: 'Entretien avec Jacques Becker', p. 12).

30   This script, also found in the BiFi archive, is very similar to the one published in *L'Avant-scène cinéma* 43 (December 1964), pp. 7–60.

31   Rivette and Truffaut: 'Entretien avec Jacques Becker', p. 12.

32   Vignaux: *Jacques Becker*, p. 124

33   Interview with Daniel Gélin, in Naumann: *Jacques Becker*, pp. 128–129.

34   Signoret: *La Nostalgie…*, p. 89. For example, see: Régent, Roger, '*Manèges*', *L'Epoque*, no date (*Manèges* dossier, CNC); Lauwick, Hervé, '*Manèges*', *Noir et Blanc*, 15 February 1950; Spade, Henri, '*Dédée d'Anvers*', *Cinémonde*, 14 September 1948; Sadoul, Georges, '*Dédée d'Anvers*: victime du poncif', *Les Lettres françaises*, 16 September 1948, p. 6; Gautier, Jean-Jacques on *Dédée d'Anvers* (1948), cited in David, Catherine, *Simone Signoret ou la mémoire partagée* (Paris: Robert Laffont, 1990), p. 74. N.B.: For articles consulted in the BiFi digitised press collection, page numbers are not usually available. They will be given whenever possible.

35   Signoret: *La Nostalgie…*, pp. 115–116.

36   Naumann: *Jacques Becker*, pp. 26, 125 and 149.

37   Vignaux: *Jacques Becker*, pp. 193–194.

38   Letter dated 23 July 1951 from Becker to Monsieur Flûry of the Crédit National, BiFi production archive.

39   Letter dated 15 June 1951 from Spéva Films to Crédit National, BiFi production archive.

40   Jeancolas, Jean-Pierre, 'Beneath the despair, the show goes on: Marcel Carné's *Les Enfants du paradis* (1943–5)', in Hayward and Vincendeau: *French Film*, pp. 78–88; and Antoine Mayo, 'Autobiographie', in Alain and Odette Virmaux, *Le Grand jeu et le cinéma: Anthologie* (Paris: Editions Paris Expérimental, with the collaboration of the Centre National du Livre, 1996), p. 113.

41   Andrew: '*Casque d'or, casquettes*', pp. 117–118.

42   See, for example, *Rendez-vous de juillet*, *Edouard et Caroline*, *Rue de l'Estrapade* and *Touchez pas au grisbi*.

43   Andrew: '*Casque d'or, casquettes*', p. 124.

44   Truffaut, François, 'Une certaine tendance du cinéma français', *Cahiers du cinéma* 31 (January 1954), pp. 15–29.

45   Truffaut: 'Une certaine tendance'. See also Baecque, Antoine de and Serge Toubiana, *François Truffaut* (Paris: Gallimard, 1997), pp. 117–118.

46   Powrie, Phil, 'Introduction: Fifteen years of 1950s cinema', *Studies in French Cinema* 4.1 (2004), pp. 5–13, pp. 6–7; Sorlin, Pierre, *European Cinemas, European Societies, 1939–1990* (London and New York: Routledge, 1991), pp. 101–102.

47   Crisp, Colin, *The Classic French Cinema 1930–1960* (London: I.B. Tauris, 1993), p. 422. See also: Burch, Noël and Geneviève Sellier, *La Drôle de guerre des sexes du cinéma français 1930–1956* (Paris: Nathan, 1996); Chapuy, Armand, *Martine Carol filmée par Christian-Jaque: Un phénomène du cinéma populaire* (Paris: Harmattan, 2001); Hayward: *Simone Signoret*; Vincendeau, Ginette, *Stars and Stardom in French Cinema* (London and New York: Continuum, 2000); and Vincendeau, Ginette, *Jean-Pierre Melville: An American in Paris* (London: BFI, 2003).

48   Andrew: '*Casque d'or, casquettes*'; Quéval, Jean, '*Casque d'or*', *Radio-Cinéma-Télévision*, 4 May 1952; Magnan, Henri, 'Le Cinéma: *Casque d'or*, de Jacques Becker', *Le Monde*, 18 April 1952; Doniol-Valcroze, Jacques, 'Les Cheveux sur la soupe', *France Observateur*, 24 April 1952.

49   Naumann: *Jacques Becker*, p. 20. Other assistants included Luchino Visconti, Henri Cartier-Bresson and Yves Allégret.

50   Andrew: '*Casque d'or, casquettes*', p. 113.

51   Even though *Les Enfants du paradis* (1943–1945) was made during the war and released after the Liberation, it is still very much inscribed within the pre-war Poetic Realist tradition.

52   Sadoul, Georges, 'Puissance de la sobriété', *L'Ecran français*, 18 April 1952.

53   Jeancolas: 'Beneath the despair', p. 79.

54   Andrew: '*Casque d'or, casquettes*', pp. 112–113.

55   Hayward, Susan, *French National Cinema* (London and New York: Routledge, 1993), p. 188.

56   Hayward: *French National Cinema*, p. 188; Burch and Sellier: *La Drôle de guerre des sexes*, p. 245.

57   From an interview with C.M. Trémois in *Télérama*, 12 February 1963, cited in Vincendeau: *Jean-Pierre Melville*, p. 153.

58   Sadoul, Georges, 'La Haine toute nue: *Caroline chérie*, un film de Jean Anouilh, Richard Pottier et Cécil Saint-Laurent', *Les Lettres françaises*, 15 March 1951, p. 6.

59   Sellier, Geneviève, 'The Belle Epoque genre in post-war French cinema: a woman's film *à la française?*', *Studies in French Cinema* 3.1 (2003), pp. 47–53.

60   Hayward: *French National Cinema*, p. 147 and Sellier: 'The Belle Epoque genre', p. 53.

61   Doniol-Valcroze, Jacques, 'Déshabillage d'une petite bourgeoise sentimentale', *Cahiers du cinéma* 31 (January 1954), pp. 2–14, p. 14.

62   Duchen, Claire, *Women's Rights and Women's Lives in France 1944–1968* (London and New York: Routledge, 1994), pp. 188–189.

63   Duchen: *Women's Rights and Women's Lives*, pp. 24–28.

64   See Brossat, Alain, *Les Tondues: Un carnaval moche* (Pereire Levallois: Manya, 1992), and Laurens, Corin, '"La Femme au turban": Les femmes tondues', in H.

R. Kedward and Nancy Wood, *The Liberation of France: Image and Event* (Oxford: Berg, 1995), pp. 155–179.

65   Burch and Sellier: *La Drôle de guerre des sexes*, p. 218.

66   Doniol-Valcroze: 'Déshabillage d'une petite bourgeoise sentimentale', pp. 2–14.

67   Doniol-Valcroze: 'Déshabillage d'une petite bourgeoise sentimentale', p. 5.

68   Burch and Sellier: *La Drôle de guerre des sexes*.

69   See also Duchen: *Women's Rights and Women's Lives*, pp. 104–105; Lehmann, Andrée, *Le Rôle de la femme française au milieu du vingtième siècle*, Third Edition (Paris: Edition de la Ligue Française pour le Droit des Femmes, 1965), p. 7.

70   The evocation of *collaboration horizontale* through these characters demonstrates the enduring legacy of wartime anxiety surrounding unruly female sexuality, real or imagined.

71   Sellier: 'The Belle Epoque genre', p. 51.

72   Sellier: 'The Belle Epoque genre', p. 51.

73   This is frequently commented on by critics in relation to Signoret's film performances, and by the 1950s Darrieux has evolved from her ingénue roles of the 1930s to play women who show a keen awareness of the often oppressive situations in which they find themselves (for example in *La Ronde*, 1950, and *La Vérité sur Bébé Donge*, 1952). Darrieux also appeared in prestige literary adaptations that could be seen to epitomise the tradition of quality: *Ruy Blas* (Billon, 1948) with Jean Marais and *Le Rouge et le noir* (Autant-Lara, 1954) with Gérard Philipe. And, in terms of the younger generation, Danièle Delorme offers an alternative to the highly sexualised *femme-enfant* star images of Brigitte Bardot and Cécile Aubry, for example.

74   See Bergstrom, Janet, 'Renouer: *French Cancan*, ou le retour de Jean Renoir en France', trans. by Christian-Marc Bosséno, *Vertigo* 21 (July 2001), pp. 157–166, on the representation of relations between men and women in this film.

75   Burch and Sellier: *La Drôle de guerre des sexes*, p. 261.

2 The film: narrative, style and ideology

Narrative structure

Casque d'or is made up of 21 sequences (plus an epilogue – the final shot of the waltzing couple), linked by the classical narrative pattern of cause and effect (see Appendix 2 for breakdown of sequences). These sequences fall into three discernable sections or movements: the Meeting, the Idyll and the Revenge. The Meeting (sequences 1–6, 44 minutes 22 seconds) can be likened to an overture in the *guinguette*, on a waltz theme, followed by an exposition which picks up tempo as we are introduced to all the major characters and witness the main events which will determine the course of the narrative. The Idyll (sequences 7–10, 22 minutes 52 seconds) is a slow movement, offering us a pause in the narrative progression – a kind of false happy ending. Finally, the Revenge (sequences 11–21, 23 minutes 56 seconds) picks up the pace once again but this time in a minor key, leading us to the crescendo of the tragic *dénouement*. In each of these three movements, certain spaces dominate: the first is situated primarily in Belleville, the second in Joinville and the third split between Belleville and the spaces controlled by the law. Given the tight links between time and space in *Casque d'or* – where different places and thus, by implication, different characters are associated with quite different temporal patterns – it might be more appropriate to use the Bakhtinian concept of the chronotope to describe these different 'worlds' across which the cause and effect narrative pattern operates.[1]

Movement, time and space

The first of these chronotopes is that of Belleville (the Ange Gabriel, the streets, Leca's house), dominated by Leca and his gang, where time is marked rigidly by appointments and routine. The second is that defined by the solid, working-class values of Danard and his workshop. Here time is evoked through the daily rhythm of work and mealtimes. A third chronotope is that connected with Joinville, Mère Eugène's farm, the riverbank, the boat in which Marie rows towards the sleeping Manda, when the couple meet up again after Roland's murder, the church and the village square. Here, the passing of time is marked by the smoking of a cigarette, or a stroll in the forest, and it seems that by slowing down movement, the passing of time can also be retarded. Minor and major characters are firmly inscribed within these *milieux* by the everyday tasks they perform there and which reveal so much about them: Manda at the lathe (hard-working and steadfast), Leca shaving, looking in the mirror or brushing his jacket (vain and self-satisfied), Mère Eugène feeding her pigs, cutting bread or hanging out her washing, or Danard performing tasks in his workshop (hard-working and kindly). Finally, there is a fourth chronotope, which is that of the law: spaces such as the police station, the prison vehicle and the prison itself. The three sections of the film are marked by particular chronotopes, and while that of Belleville dominates, occurring in all three sections, the more marginal spaces can be said to have a greater effect on the mood of each section, precisely because they do not feature in the rest of the film. So, the second section is heralded by a transitional opening sequence, which ends with Danard closing the door of his *atelier* having watched Manda walk away from his life as a carpenter. We then fade into Manda arriving at Mère Eugène's farm, where this second section will also close – a rural sanctuary that has already been evoked in the opening sequence at the *guinguette* (the riverside café and dance hall) – while the final section is dominated by the spaces of the law, which have also been prefigured, this time by the intrusion of the police at the Ange Gabriel at the end of the first section.

Like all classical narrative films, *Casque d'or* is structured according to a linear cause and effect logic that drives it from sequence to sequence towards its conclusion. The narrative pattern of the film is linear: we progress from the meeting of Marie and Manda via its various consequences – Roland's humiliation, Marie's visit to Manda, Manda's offer to Marie, the fight between Roland and Manda, and so on – until we reach Manda's revenge on Leca and his execution. The narrative is driven forward by the desires of Marie and Manda but is complicated by the conflicting desires of Leca. Desires prompt characters to act and, especially, to move, causing them to step out of their usual environment and enter another, provoking a sort of chronotopic clash – the major source of tension in the film. Marie's visit to Manda at Danard's workshop is clearly an intrusion – she cannot penetrate the interior and meets Manda on the wasteground in front of the boutique. Likewise, Manda's visit to the Ange Gabriel is a provocation from which the fatal fight with Roland ensues. And later, Leca will step out of his normal environment, donning the guise of a weekend fisherman (even though, as Marie remarks, it is not Sunday), going to Joinville to break the news of Raymond's arrest to Manda.

Certain characters, then, are firmly located within a particular space, while others, like Leca, have a clear base from which they extend their influence. However, in Marie's case, she does not have a zone to leave, since she refuses to occupy the space designated for her. As Roland's 'girl', *she* rows the boat, and though she gives in and dances with him she does manage to avoid sharing his bed, staying at Julie's place instead. And after Roland's death, she again beats a hasty retreat with Julie in order to avoid sharing Leca's. Marie, it seems, is not inscribed within any particular space. Of all the characters, she is the one most associated with transport: particularly carriages and boats. This is the case from the very first sequence, when she is the only woman of the group to be rowing, to the later scene, when she silently approaches Manda who is sleeping on the riverbank, contemplating him from her boat, and from the moment she takes a cab to visit Manda at his workshop to that when she instructs the cab driver to get her to the prison where Manda and Raymond are being taken. This association with movement not only emphasises the fact that Marie is a woman of action, but also suggests that she is obliged to keep moving until she finds her own place – a space where she would be free from the power exerted by those who wish to contain her. The fact that Marie visits all spaces but belongs to none of them also demonstrates her lack of fixity – as is suggested by her association with the river, she is a character in flux (like Manda, once he has abandoned his home in Danard's workshop). Though this could be said in one way to parallel her status as object of exchange between men, Marie can in fact be seen to use this fluid positioning to her advantage, refusing to be pinned down. So, just when Leca believes he owns her, she escapes him – emotionally through her attachment to Manda, and physically by managing to leave with Julie in the nick of time. This lack of fixity – something Susan Hayward argues is a key element of Signoret's star persona – extends also to her gender identity, as we shall see later on.[2]

The temporal progression of the film is clearly indicated with the use of 'punctuation' – fades in and out are used to indicate a new day, or a transition from daytime to evening, while wipes and dissolves are more likely to show simultaneity, or at least temporal contiguity. In this apparently effortless way, Becker maintains the rigorous narrative structure of the film, set over just a few days, but with significant variations in pace. In each chronotope, as already mentioned, time passes differently: varying the rhythm of the film, and the way time itself is represented, calling attention to the relationship between movement and time. To compare two different chronotopes, in Belleville, time is referred to in the dialogue predominantly in the future tense, dominated by Leca's demands on his gang to be in a specific place at a specific time. Marie is to give him her answer that evening at the Ange Gabriel. In Joinville, on the other hand, the couple live for the immediate present: their rather sparse dialogue refers to what is happening in the here and now ('Is there any coffee?' 'Kiss me, Manda.' 'It's a wedding, let's go and have a look.') and Marie searches the room for reassuring indictors of Manda's presence upon her awakening. (Of course, on the last morning, when their idyll has been interrupted, Manda has gone, and the time references become past tense: 'He left an hour ago.')

Camera movements are also temporal indicators. When Marie approaches Manda from the river, the camera, positioned on a boat, tracks forward with her towards the sleeping Manda. This is movement in more or less real time, whereas, at the end of the sequence, camera movement is used to introduce a simultaneous sequence – a visual 'meanwhile'. In a remarkable transition, the camera tilts upwards to frame the trees above Marie and Manda in the forest. There is then a cut to some different trees, before the camera reverses its movement, tilting back down to earth, to reveal Leca striding along the Belleville street, accompanied by his jaunty theme, introducing the sequence in which he will betray Raymond, putting an end to the lovers' rural idyll.

This juxtaposing of different temporal patterns is also important in that timing is crucial to the plot of *Casque d'or*. When Leca demands an answer from Marie, she, believing Manda to be lost to her, agrees to become his girl. In the next second, before Leca has had the chance to greet his *apaches*, let alone speak to Roland about Marie, Manda arrives: 'I've come for you, Marie.' But he is too late: Manda is led to believe that in fighting Roland he can win her, and only Marie and Leca know that this is no longer the case. This is the timing of tragedy, evoking a spectator response of 'if only . . .'. However, this is no tragedy of fate, there is no *deus ex machina* causing Manda's timing to be out. The clear establishment of the different chronotopes and their association with particular characters means that we already know that, in Belleville (and that includes the Ange Gabriel), it is Leca who determines the temporal logic, by keeping all those who answer to his authority on a tight rein. Manda is an intruder here, posing a threat to this absolute authority, though he does not know it yet.

Oedipal triangles

The ordering of time and space, then, is crucial to the narrative structure of the film with respect to its effect on the characters: on their relationships with each other and on their actions, driven as we have seen, by hunger for power as well as sexual desire. The challenge posed by Manda to Leca's authority can be seen in Oedipal terms, Manda's desire for Marie, the female other, conflicting with that of the 'father', Leca.[3] Viewed in this way, the meeting between Marie and Manda can be seen as evocative of Lacan's mirror stage of development. Just like the (male) infant becoming aware of his mirror image for the first time and misrecognising it as himself, Manda experiences his first encounter with Marie as a moment of *jouissance*, of imaginary unity with the (m)other, a moment of plenitude whose passing creates a lack that needs to be filled (see Figure 1). This is reinforced first by the look of the other (Raymond), who first identifies Manda as an old friend and then witnesses the exchange of looks between the dancing Marie and the watching Manda, and secondly by the series of close-ups alternating on first her and then his face as he is

Figure 1: The mutual gaze: Marie and Manda's meeting, a moment of *jouissance*.

leaving, which could be seen as extricating the couple from their environment and situating them in the Imaginary space of *jouissance*. The lighting in these close-ups of their faces creates halo effects and the camera uses soft focus to detach the shots from the rest of the sequence, which is characterised by deep focus, sharp images and a lack of any impressionistic lighting. It is almost as if Becker wishes to return to silent cinema with these shots, preferring to show us the birth of Marie and Manda's passion by purely visual means.

Becker claimed that one reason for the film's poor reception was its 'abundance of dead time', suggesting an absence of movement.[4] In fact, as Jean-Louis Tarnowski has pointed out, there are very few 'temps morts' and the narrative progresses rapidly along its cause and effect chain, gathering pace in the final part.[5] So these alternating close-ups of Marie and Manda, then, when time appears to stop, would seem to stand out in the film, returning to this moment of *jouissance*. This is all the more evident since these alternating close-ups marked by soft focus, short focal length and glamorous lighting effects – especially on Signoret – recur three times in the film: firstly, at the end of their first meeting; secondly, when they meet again outside the carpenter's workshop; and, finally, when Marie awakens Manda on the riverbank in Joinville. If the narrative corresponds to the Oedipal drive of the male subject to assume his role within the Symbolic order, ultimately leading to the tragic ending, these shots represent the desire to return to the Imaginary, to this moment of *jouissance*. For Marie and Manda, this goal is twice achieved and twice interrupted: the first time, when Marie goes to find Manda at Danard's workshop, their reunion is postponed by the actions of Léonie; and the second time, their Joinville idyll is abruptly terminated by the news Leca brings of Raymond's arrest. And, indeed, the final shot of the waltzing couple twirling into the distance in a now empty *guinguette* – belonging outside the film's narrative chronotopes – can be seen as the ultimate triumph of the Imaginary.

Manda has certainly been viewed as an Oedipal hero, following in the footsteps of the tragic popular hero of 1930s Poetic Realism.[6] In many ways, he fits the bill, leaving behind the good father (Danard) to do battle with the bad father (Leca) over the female other, Marie, and tragically paying for his challenge to patriarchal order with his life (the symbolism of the guillotine as an instrument of castration is hardly subtle). And Leca is presented as the embodiment of patriarchal authority: he manipulates the law through 'his' corrupt policeman, disciplines his gang through punishment and reward, and, if need be, takes the law into his own hands (Anatole's murder).

However, such a reading privileges the patriarchal aspect of the film, whereas, in fact, there are plenty of ways in which *Casque d'or* challenges this. The most obvious of these is the character of Marie, who cannot be reduced to a passive Oedipal role, for she too is a desiring and active subject in this narrative. Indeed, *Casque d'or* is far from the Oedipal model of 1930s French cinema identified by Ginette Vincendeau.[7] Marie is endowed with an active gaze with the power to eroticise and we often share her point of view. For example: it is she who first notices Manda and initiates the exchange of looks with him at the *guinguette*; she spots Billy and Ponsard arriving at Julie's room looking for her before they know she is hiding there; we share her perspective of Manda sleeping on the riverside as she rows her boat towards him; and finally, the intercutting of close-ups of Marie during the execution sequence ensures that this too is rendered from her point of view. And Marie, as we have seen above, escapes the confines that patriarchal society sets out for her, hiding from Roland at the beginning of the film, and slipping through Leca's hands at the end of the first part, just at the very moment when he is bragging to his friends about his 'conquest'. We begin and end the film with Marie, thus ensuring that Manda's tale comes to us through her eyes, in a reversal of the numerous contemporary films in which women are narrated by men, often 'victims' of their 'charms'.[8]

If Marie's desire dominates the first section of the film, in the second section, she and Manda are presented as equal subjects: their bodies are constructed as both desiring and desired. This is shown principally through the structuring of the look in the Joinville sequences, which will be discussed more fully in the final part of this chapter, 'A feminist film?' This equality between the two protagonists is a second reason that the Oedipal structure does not fit *Casque d'or*. A third reason is that, rather than following the usual Oedipal trajectory of the main (male) character towards 'adult' masculinity, here both protagonists can be seen as already formed subjects at the beginning of the film: Manda has now reformed after his term in jail, and is engaged to the somewhat dour Léonie, while Marie is on the lookout for someone to replace the snivelling Roland, of whom she has grown tired.[9]

The final third of the film shows the response of patriarchal society to this challenge to its authority. Leca, the father figure who has been so easily dismissed by the couple, is not about to relinquish his power so easily. However, in order to defeat this mutual, equal desire, he must pervert the structures of patriarchal authority – the code of honour that he has upheld in his gang – and in doing so, he seals his own fate, allowing moral authority to pass to Manda (see Figure 2). It is not just anyone that Leca betrays, it is Raymond, the embodiment of loyalty and masculine friendship. Up to now, desire has been the motivating force of the narrative. From now on, this motivation is split between the couple's mutual desire and the implacable drive of Manda's revenge, until the couple is reunited in the final shot of their waltz. This empty *guinguette* is a dream-like space of *jouissance* for Marie and Manda. Such is the weight of patriarchal oppression, the film appears to say, that only in such an Imaginary space can a truly equal partnership exist. Manda's destruction of Leca has revealed the vulnerability of the father figure, and this is why he must be punished. What is perhaps most remarkable for the time is that for all its fairytale romance, *Casque d'or* remains firmly rooted in a realist cinematic tradition, drawing on Renoir and looking ahead to the New Wave. The following section will examine this realism in greater detail, focusing on locations and costumes.

Authenticity, elegance and the costume drama

'In general, I've no real interest in the exceptional. I've never been able to get very excited about stories where the heroes are criminals; their situation doesn't attract me…'[10] If Becker is to be taken at his word, and the majority of the films he made up to this point suggest that he should be, then his interest in *Casque d'or* – a melodrama set among the criminal classes in Belle Epoque Belleville – seems hard to fathom. *Casque d'or* may be a costume film – a genre more often associated with spectacle, eroticism and melodrama – but in its

Figure 2: Manda borrows the arm of the law to exact his revenge on Leca.

consistent focus on the everyday, ordinary activities of its characters it firmly renounces the spectacular in favour of a sober, understated realism.

At the time of *Casque d'or*, the model for cinematic realism came from Italian cinema. Much has been written elsewhere on Italian neo-realism so the debates surrounding it will not be covered in any detail here.[11] What is most interesting for our discussion of *Casque d'or* is that Becker was singled out as France's answer to neo-realism, thanks mainly to his focus on contemporary society and his portrayal of social classes beyond the bourgeoisie.[12] For this reason, it is worth considering very briefly two contemporary responses to post-war Italian cinema: that of the Communist critic Georges Sadoul and that of André Bazin. Sadoul hailed the neo-realist focus on contemporary social problems such as poverty and unemployment, placing the emphasis on 'social' realism, the depiction of the working classes in their own environment. André Bazin, on the other hand, praised the neo-realist aesthetic, arguing that '[r]ealism in art can only be achieved in one way – through artifice', so all that could be hoped for is an image that is mediated as little as possible.[13] The neo-realists' preference for long takes and deep focus over montage, Bazin argued, replicated reality more closely, by enabling spectators to choose what to focus on within the frame.[14] *Casque d'or*, then, would seem to correspond to neither of these definitions of realism. Becker's film may have a working-class hero, but – as Sadoul pointed out – it is not concerned primarily with workers' rights. Neither is it a model of Bazinian realist aesthetics: although Becker does use deep-focus photography and some location shooting, he is also famous for his highly edited films, and *Casque d'or* is no exception.

Elegance and editing

From the 1930s, French classical cinema was characterised by longer takes than Hollywood films. As both Colin Crisp and Ginette Vincendeau note, though, French editing rates increased from the mid-1930s to the 1950s, and average shot lengths (ASLs) declined from 15 seconds in the mid-1930s to around 9.5 in the post-war years.[15] However, as Ginette Vincendeau points out, the costume drama is a general exception to this rule: she cites a range of between 10.2 seconds (*French Cancan*) and 19 seconds (*Les Misérables*, Jean-Paul Le Chanois, 1958).[16] Even by 1950s standards, however, many of Becker's films were judged to have a remarkably high edit rate (the most 'notorious' was *Antoine et Antoinette* with an ASL of approximately 5 seconds, though *Edouard et Caroline* with 8.3 seconds was more in keeping with the norms).[17] *Casque d'or*'s ASL of 8.1 seconds approaches the general norm for 1950s French films, but is much shorter than other costume dramas. A closer look at the film (see Appendix 2) reveals that the middle section, dominated by the Joinville sequences, has a longer rate (11 seconds – closer to the costume drama norm), while the first and final sections, where there is a higher concentration of action sequences, have quicker ASLs (respectively 7.4 seconds and 7.1 seconds). The gathering pace of the narrative towards the end of the film corresponds to a series of much shorter sequences, with ASLs that are often much quicker than the film's average, until the climax of Leca's shooting. The pace then slows once again for the execution sequence. The importance of movement in the film in determining the narrative pace has already been highlighted and these figures would seem to back this up, with clusters of shorter takes corresponding to moments of greater action, and with the slowest rate at the moment when Manda realises that he is trapped (sequence 10).

Vincendeau points out the aesthetic effects of the French preference for longer takes: close-ups and shot/reverse shot patterns, which abound in Hollywood film and which privilege the individual, are rejected in favour of longer shots framing two or three characters at a time to portray conversations, or shots featuring the group. French cinema, then, tends to give greater emphasis to the representation of communities. Even if Becker shows a preference for shorter takes, in this cinema of community he is no exception: *Casque d'or* uses ensemble shots to depict the group, often contrasting these with close-ups or medium close-ups that isolate an individual. For example, when Marie dances with Manda at the *guinguette*, close-ups of a furious Roland are intercut with long shots of the group. Becker collaborated closely with his editor, Marguerite Houllé-Renoir, experimenting in the cutting room to give his films a polished and elegant style. Although he cut more than his contemporaries (with the exception of René Clément), Becker used movement – of the camera and of actors – to retain an impression of a flowing narrative. This is especially marked in punctuation between scenes or sequences. For example, during the search for Marie in the second sequence, wipes introduce each new set of characters, moving in the same direction as the characters, connecting the scenes temporally and through the object of their search, and emphasising the distance the characters cover in their search. The opening and closing of doors frequently figure as punctuation too: Manda's departure from Danard's workshop is represented as Danard returns inside, closing the door behind him – a dissolve introduces the next sequence with Manda arriving at Mère Eugène's farm. But later on when Manda is hunting Leca down, doors open and close with much more dynamic effect, linking the two characters. Manda, frustrated not to find Leca at home, slams the door as he leaves, and the next shot shows Leca opening the door of the Ange Gabriel, to find his gang gathered around the dying Raymond. The link between the two characters is further reinforced by the fact that the last person to come through that door was Manda, in search of Leca and a doctor for the wounded Raymond. This matching of shots through movement is a characteristic of Becker's elegantly flowing style of film-making, which Alain Resnais described as giving a 'sensation of suppleness', and the source of the refinement and charm of Becker's films.[18]

This elegance can also be seen in the framing and staging of shots: for example, when Frédo informs Leca of Marie and Manda's whereabouts, we clearly see Raymond reflected in the mirror behind the two characters, his ear in the centre of the frame, just as Frédo confidently assures Leca that no one can overhear them. Later on, it is once again Raymond (now dead) who occupies the centre of the frame in the background when Leca arrives at the Ange Gabriel, only to be confronted with the accusing stares of his gang members, and the realisation that, if Raymond is dead, a vengeful Manda will not be far away.

Becker puts this meticulous style at the service of a realist conception of cinema rooted in the quotidian. These gangsters are not featured performing dramatic bank robberies (though they do share out the proceeds of a previous coup), but rather playing cards, meeting for lunch or getting dressed in the morning. This is where the notion of 'authenticity' comes into play – in the film's focus on the ordinary – ordinary people, ordinary activities and ordinary places – at a time when the vast majority of films focus exclusively on the wealthy upper-middle classes. Becker also consistently foregrounds the ordinary at moments of melodrama or action. Manda's fight with Roland is as far as it could possibly be from either the newspaper reports of the *apaches'* gun battles and knife attacks, or from the blade-flourishing of films such as *Fanfan la tulipe*. The use of close-ups during this fight de-spectacularises the violence, reducing movement to a minimum and focusing on the straining faces of the two opponents. And Roland's final agony is rendered only by the image of his hand falling from Manda's face, turning his gouging grip into a soft caress.

Minor characters also function to decentre attention at moments of dramatic tension. For example, when Marie first goes to see Manda, provoking the conflict with Léonie, her visit is paralleled by the arrival of a customer who broke his table by sitting on it. Later, as she anxiously awaits Manda and Raymond's arrival at the prison, her cab driver relieves himself against the wall. This focus on secondary characters, even extremely minor roles – what Bazin might call a 'fundamentally humanist' treatment of characters – inscribes the protagonists firmly within a social environment and recalls Renoir's collective film-making of the 1930s.[19] Becker was also known for the meticulousness of his *mise-en-scène*, but in *Casque d'or* it is these characters who inhabit the sets, bringing them to life far more effectively than any obsessive re-creation of detail.

Locations

Also like Renoir in the 1930s, Becker went against the trends of the time in preferring location shooting, central to the authenticity of the film.[20] In *Casque d'or*, Belleville street scenes, Leca's villa, Danard's workshop, and the Joinville scenes (actually shot in Annet-sur-Marne) offer a record of Paris and its outskirts in the early 1950s. Given the development of that part of the twentieth district of Paris since that decade, especially the construction of high-rise, low-cost housing, many of the streets are now unrecognisable. However, in addition to preserving an image of the district as parts of it were, *Casque d'or* has also provided a legacy of actual conservation. Number 44, rue des Cascades – Leca's villa in the film – was granted a preservation order in 1992 after protests against plans to build a block of flats on the site were upheld.[21] This site is marked by nostalgia on many levels: for the legendary *faubourg* of the *apaches* and the *grisettes*; for Marie and Manda's tragically short love affair; but also for a Belleville invested with the glamour of cinema and its stars; and finally, for a neighbourhood as yet untouched by the development of large *cités* (estates). This enduring impact of the film on this area is also shown by the fact that the rue des Cascades now boasts a restaurant named … '*Casque d'or*'.

The use of real locations means that *Casque d'or* has left its mark on Paris in a way that the majority of studio-shot films of its time could not. There is a difference between the use of these exteriors in the urban and the rural scenes, however. In the Paris scenes, where the interiors are frequently filmed in constructed sets, exterior shots function primarily to establish the relationship between the different spaces of the film in relation to each other, and the environment in which the characters live, and go about their daily business. Therefore, they also 'authenticate' those sequences filmed on Jean d'Eaubonne's sets at the Billancourt studios, which include the Ange Gabriel, its courtyard and the surrounding streets.[22]

In the central Joinville sequences, exteriors play a different role. Here, they do not just have an 'authenticating' function: instead they make up the greatest part of the sequences, portraying the 'natural' world where Manda and Marie's love finds expression. In this world, interior shots are infrequent and, in the case of the wedding scene, are also shot in 'real' locations. As for Mère Eugène and her farm, she 'lives' outside, feeding the pigs, doing her washing and making the morning coffee – and only enters the house in order to sleep. This is the traditional idyllic space located outside of social relations, which offers their love room to blossom – that is, of course, until Leca intrudes upon them. The association of Marie and Manda's love affair with this rural setting and the open air emphasises the fact that their love cannot be contained (by Leca, in particular) and characterises it as being as natural as the setting in which it is played out.[23] For example, when Marie and Manda are walking in the forest the scene is introduced with a long shot establishing their closeness to the environment – Marie listens intently to the birds, while Manda whittles his stick. Dappled sunlight plays on Marie's hair, skin and blouse as she sits under the tree, picking a blade of grass and placing it in her mouth. Even the highly poetic backlighting of the close-ups of Marie, which illuminates her golden hair like a halo, is justified according to the laws of 'real' perception, as this is Manda's point of view, looking up towards Marie with the sun behind her. The sensuality of nature is emphasised through the association of sound and image: in the birdsong, the gentle splashes made by the oars and in the sounds of the characters' clothes brushing against the long grass as they move. These sequences clearly show the influence of location on the representation of the body and of desire as natural, as 'authentic' (see Figure 3). This authenticity (and conversely, the lack of it) is also conveyed through clothing and its relationship to the body.

Figure 3: Natural desire in a pastoral setting: Marie awakens Manda with a kiss.

Costume and the body

As with locations, clothing in *Casque d'or* does not function in the usual spectacular way of 1950s costume drama, by drawing attention to itself and the past, although it does eroticise Signoret's body, as we shall see. Signoret has described the effect of clothing in relation to her first professional experience of 'le dédoublement' (dual personality): '[I]t wasn't myself I was dressing – me, Montand's wife and Catherine's mother – it was Marie, who was already thinking about what she would wear that evening to go out with Manda…'[24]

According to Signoret, Marie manifests herself through her desire for Manda, a desire expressed through her choice of clothing. This relates to the way clothes have been seen as playing a performative role in the formation and communication of identity. As Joanne Entwistle puts it: 'It seems almost a cliché to insist that fashion and dress operate on the body and that by implication, the body and dress are now a crucial arena for the performance and articulation of identities.'[25] In an earlier work, Stella Bruzzi adds a gendered dimension to this argument, citing James Laver, who has identified

> two polarised principles: the hierarchical and the seductive. The former is applicable to men because 'a man's clothes are a function of his relation to society' whilst the latter pertains to women because 'a woman's clothes are a function of her relation to man'.[26]

However, this traditional gender division is not adequate to discuss the ways in which clothing is used to produce identity in *Casque d'or*. These principles are complicated in Becker's film: firstly by the collapsing of the female erotic and social functions (as a prostitute Marie's job is to seduce); secondly by the eroticising of the male body (Manda); and thirdly by the narcissistic preening of Leca and his gang members, for whom clothes are much more than purely functional.

Marie's costume has been discussed in relation to her sexuality and power of seduction.[27] Hayward has analysed her belt – a replacement for her absent corset – as offering an ironic commentary on 'masculine desire and power', demonstrating simultaneously Marie's awareness of her social positioning and her refusal to conform to this position (see Figure 1).[28] She sports the outward token of male power, but underneath her clothes, she remains free.

Marie's belt is not her only accessory to bear meaning: the black onyx choker she wears under her boa at the Ange Gabriel signifies her performance as the *femme fatale* (see Figure 4). Her boa – emblematic of her status as a prostitute – is exchanged for a grey shawl in later sequences, which functions variously as veil (when she and Manda enter the church to look at the wedding, she covers her head with it) and shroud (she wears it wrapped tightly round her body as she watches over Manda's execution).

The interplay between clothes and the body is a key contributor to *Casque d'or*'s authenticity, since the impression is not one of highly ornate and frilly fashions of the Belle Epoque as seen, for example, in *Olivia* (Audry, 1951), but rather of a more solid corporeality. This is shown in part through movement – Signoret's firm, striding walk in particular, which causes her skirts to swish, and the way she places her hands on her hips, simultaneously emphasising her curves and demonstrating her character's determination. Signoret's body is barely contained by her clothes, appearing to almost burst upwards from her slim waist to her full bosom and shoulders, culminating in her crowning glory, her magnificent hair piled up on top of her head. Signoret's body is shown as soft and inviting – the roundness of her breasts and shoulders emphasised by blouses with plunging necklines that slip off her shoulders. However, her hairstyle – the gleaming helmet for which Marie is famous – gives an impression of shining armour, carefully dyed and constructed to present a hard surface. Marie only lets her hair down when she is in bed with Manda, and in these shots it is presented as soft and luxuriant, with a much warmer glow than the dazzling reflective surface it presents in earlier sequences. Marie's '*casque*' has a double function: a weapon

Figure 4: Marie's masquerade: she gives in to Leca under Julie's gaze.

she deploys to entrap men, and a shield for her own protection. She rarely lets her guard down – even in her underwear in Julie's room, her hair is in place and her hairbrush in her hand. It is significant, then, that when she is faced with Leca's ultimatum, the extreme close-up of her tear-stained face cuts off her magnificent hair – Marie is now without defences. And in the execution sequence, her hair lacks its usual carefully groomed smoothness. Picked out by street lighting, the lamp in the stairwell and the candle in the bedroom, Marie's hair shines like the blade of the guillotine, or Manda's white shirt. However, in the cold light of dawn, when she bows her head at the moment the blade falls, its gleam has dulled – her '*casque*' is no longer either weapon or shield.

Let us turn now to the male characters. Manda's costume reveals more of his body than those of the *apaches*. Even when Leca is shaving, his body is fully covered. Manda, on the other hand, often wears his shirt unbuttoned and sleeves rolled up – these are clothes that allow athletic movements. The wide band around the waist, the loose corduroy trousers and the cap on his head mark him out as a carpenter, and so apparently conform to Laver's principle, suggesting that men's clothes – and therefore male identity – are defined by their social activity. However, when Manda leaves Danard's, he exchanges his tie for a check cotton scarf he wears knotted around his neck, with the top buttons of his shirt undone. Susan Hayward has argued that Manda's clothes construct 'an interesting unfixed image of masculinity',[29] contrasting with the rigidity of the other male clothing (of the *apaches*, or the bourgeois visitors to the Ange Gabriel). Manda's gender identity shifts: on occasion his body is eroticised through the adoption of a more 'feminine' (to-be-looked-at) position, signalled through costume, or rather, the lack of it. For example, when Marie and Manda awake after their first night of lovemaking, the script notes that Marie is 'visibly naked under the sheet' and that Manda is 'bare-chested'.[30] However, though Reggiani's wiry upper body is offered for the spectator's contemplation, Signoret is in fact wearing a nightdress. Much as Signoret's body gains sensuality because it is not laced into a corset, so does Reggiani's through these images of the body beneath the soft fabrics of his costume. This impression of corporeality lends a further dimension to the film's sensuality and authenticity. Manda's full moustache also links the body directly to costume, as an indication of 'natural' masculinity compared with that of the *apaches* (whose rather effete moustaches are clipped and waxed). Truffaut, of course, highlighted Manda's moustache as the emblem of *Casque d'or*'s authenticity.[31]

Clothes differentiate Manda and Danard (and also Raymond, indicating his solidarity with his working friend) from the *apaches* they encounter at the *guinguette*, who wear loud check suits, with the jacket open but for the top button, in order to show off their patterned waistcoats and ties (see Figure 5). These flashy clothes go with their ostentatious behaviour, in the tradition of the gangster film, but also following the descriptions of the original *apaches*. Court reports describe Manda as looking the part of 'the elegant *souteneur*': 'His chin, clean shaven, is held high by his wing collar and his jacket of fine grey cloth is of an irreproachable cut.'[32] In the fight scene between Manda and Roland, Roland flamboyantly throws off his bowler hat, adopting melo-dramatic postures, while Manda remains almost still, quietly folding his cap and placing it in his pocket. The gesture is full of the quiet confidence he has manifested in all his confrontations with Roland up to now: he is sure he will need his cap later, and he will not give it up for the bowler hat that Leca imposes on his *apaches*.

Raymond, the loyal friend, is shown as having an uneasy relationship to the sartorial codes of the *milieu* – his cap symbolises his solidarity with Manda, and thus his authenticity (see Figure 5). On the other hand, Leca and Roland are the most narcissistic of the gangsters. Roland's vanity is shown through his sobriquet, 'Belle gueule' (Pretty Face), while Leca is constantly attending to his appearance or looking in the mirror. Bruzzi argues that the screen gangster is defined by his narcissism, 'manifested by a preoccupation with the appearance of others and a self-conscious regard for his own'.[33] For

Figure 5: Carpenter versus *apache:* Manda and Raymond wear the cap of the working man.

Leca, who poses as an 'honest' wine merchant, appearance is what counts: he berates Raymond and Billy for wearing caps and not hats (what will the neighbours say?). His own costume (pinstriped suits, patterned waistcoats and striped shirts) and the ostentatious decoration of his house attest to his superficiality and lack of authenticity. Ultimately, his patriarchal stance is revealed as nothing but a masquerade: his narcissism is too dysfunctional to allow him to occupy the place of the father and so, he has no chance faced with Manda's authentic masculinity at the end.

Marie and Manda's clothes also showcase the sensuality of their mutually desiring bodies. The *apaches*, on the other hand, especially Leca, do not experience authentic desire, only a narcissistic drive that is reflected back onto the self. Leca may think he wants Marie, but he always ends up looking in the mirror. His is not a comfortable body image, like that of Marie and Manda, it is a misrecognition of his power, projected onto his dapper reflection. *Casque d'or*, then, is a costume film that is concerned with the representation of desiring bodies. Crucial to any discussion of the representation of these bodies must be the questions of stardom and performance, and so it is to these that we now turn.

Stardom and performance

In her autobiography, Simone Signoret recounts a discussion she had with Henri-Georges Clouzot during the filming of *Les Diaboliques* (Clouzot, 1955):

> I had never impressed him, and my talent, if I had any, had never caught his attention. He had considered *Casque d'or* as a 'non-film', and had scientifically demonstrated to me how it could have become a film if he, Clouzot had directed it instead of Jacques … with Martine Carol in the title role.[34]

What is certain is that Martine Carol's Casque d'or would have been radically different from the character interpreted by Signoret. Carol's appeal depended on her apparent availability to all, and in the face of competition from younger stars (Brigitte Bardot) Carol worked hard to maintain her profile. Perhaps her Casque d'or, then, would have been closer to the original, Amélie Hélie, who also sought to capitalise on her notoriety. This is a far cry from Signoret's Marie: a sensual, proud woman who finds fulfilment not as the gang's most desirable prostitute, but through her love for a quiet carpenter.

This imaginary substitution of Carol for Signoret demonstrates the importance of stars in bringing meaning to a film. While stars are most often associated with Hollywood movies, they are also of crucial economic importance to French cinema, and indeed, offer domestic films a way of competing with American imports. Their significance is not solely economic, though: stars also bear cultural and social meaning. Arguably, the meaning of *Casque d'or* – its legend – is bound up closely with Signoret's star 'myth': with what she embodied for audiences in 1952, and, for more recent spectators, what she has come to signify since then. Although Reggiani and Dauphin were also well known at this time, Signoret was the only star of international importance in *Casque d'or*. Ginette Vincendeau defines major stars as 'those singled out over the years by the magnitude of their box office success and their cultural resonance', and she cites Signoret among the candidates for this A-list.[35] We must therefore distinguish between the impact of her presence in the film and that of her male co-performers, and so we shall first turn to Signoret, before examining the star personas of Reggiani and Dauphin.

Signoret

Simone Signoret, born in Wiesbaden in occupied Germany in 1921, and brought up in the wealthy Paris suburb of Neuilly, emerged as a star in the post-war period, having worked as an extra on many films during the Occupation (her half-Jewish status meant she was unable to obtain a full work permit). She was first and foremost a film actress: she had very little to do with the theatre and the extent of her training was to attend acting classes with Solange Sicard, run by the Pathé studio, which aimed to replicate the American studio system by producing a stable of actors under contract.

In the early part of the war, Signoret had worked as a secretary at the collaborationist newspaper, *Les Nouveaux temps*. However, in 1941, she began to frequent the Café de Flore in Saint-Germain-des-Prés, the haunt of Picasso, Sartre and de Beauvoir among others, and left her job. It was at the Flore that she met Yves Allégret, with whom she had two children (her son died in early infancy), as well as making four films, including her two most important early roles: in *Dédée d'Anvers* (1948) and *Manèges* (1950). These extremely bleak films are part of a trilogy that is now held up as an example of the genre of 'black realism' that emerged in France in the immediate post-war years (the middle film is *Une si jolie petite plage*, 1949, starring Gérard Philipe). As we have seen, these films are emblematic of the virulent misogyny of French cinema of this time. They also influenced the development of Signoret's screen persona: she had played main parts in 11 films by the time of *Casque d'or*, and though in fact she only played prostitutes in three of them (*Macadam*, Blistène, 1946; *Dédée d'Anvers* and *La Ronde*) and an out-and-out 'garce' in one (*Manèges*), this was the image that stuck to her in this early part of her career. However, there is more to Signoret than this: in fact, she embodies a complex image of femininity.

Though she was extremely beautiful in her youth, Signoret never conformed to ideals of feminine beauty: off-screen she wore little make-up and dressed in slacks. She had long, slim legs, but she was tall and broad-shouldered – and this was remarked upon in relation to her pairing with the slight Reggiani. Her face too is a mixture of feminine and masculine traits: her wide eyes, rounded cheeks and full lips contrast with her strong jawline and determined chin. This gender complexity is a key aspect of Signoret's star image, leading to comparisons between her and Jean Gabin.[36] It is certainly the case that, in early films such as *Dédée d'Anvers* and *L'Impasse des deux anges* (Tourneur, 1948), Signoret takes on the central role and an active narrative positioning that has more in common with Gabin's 1930s roles than with those of Arletty, Michèle Morgan or Viviane Romance (though, unlike Gabin's characters, she has a tendency to survive). These comparisons are especially interesting given that a version of *Casque d'or* had been planned before the war with Gabin as Manda. As Georges Sadoul points out, such a film would surely have placed the emphasis firmly on the tragedy of the male hero, and so it can be argued that Signoret's presence in Becker's film shifts the gender balance towards the female protagonist.[37]

Signoret does not fit easily into any of the typical female stereotypes of the time: erotic *femme-objet*; 'garce' in the tradition of Viviane Romance; sophisticate *à la* Michèle Morgan, Danielle Darrieux or Edwige Feuillère; or *femme-enfant* (Danièle Delorme, Françoise Arnoul and, of course, Brigitte Bardot). There are contradictions at the heart of Signoret's star appeal: she plays prostitutes, but she is not easily 'available'; she is equally convincing as conniving bitch or great lover. Her voice – not theatrically trained – can range from tough Parisian '*gouaille*' (bold repartee) to vulnerable tenderness – always retaining a slight lisp and an element 'of the people' that keeps her performances rooted in the real – not for Signoret the brilliant verbal panache of Martine Carol or the theatrical declamations of Edwige Feuillère. The minimalism of her performances marked her out for cinema: she was known for her ability to express depths of emotion through her eyes, or with only the slightest gesture. And her characters are remarkable for their intelligence and their consistent agencing of desire.

Film roles and training are only one part of a star's persona. Publicity and gossip are equally important elements in determining their cultural meaning. Even as early as 1952, Signoret was known for her left-wing political sympathies: in addition to frequenting left-wing intellectuals in the Latin quarter, she was a signatory of the 1950 Stockholm appeal for nuclear disarmament (a move that cost her a Hollywood contract). She was a reticent star (indeed, she always refused the term), giving few interviews and protecting her daughter, Catherine, from the press, and as a result, she appears only infrequently in such popular film magazines of the time as *Cinémonde* and *Pour vous*. When she does appear outside of articles directly connected with her films, it is in connection with her relationship with Yves Montand. In 1949, Signoret left Allégret for Montand. The couple were married in 1951 at the Colombe d'or, and remained so until Signoret's death in 1985, in spite of Montand's extremely public affair with Marilyn Monroe in 1960. In the early fifties, Signoret and Montand were the ideal couple – something like the Bacall and Bogart of French cinema. Her off-screen situation, then, as part of this 'great' love affair, would have clearly affected the reception of her performance as Marie, and, according to Signoret herself, also her actual performance.[38] Before going into more detail about this, however, let us first turn our attention to Signoret's co-stars.

Serge Reggiani and Claude Dauphin

Serge Reggiani was born in Reggio nell'Emilia in Italy in 1922, but moved to France with his family in order to escape the Mussolini regime. The son of a barber, he contemplated first boxing then cycling as professions before enrolling at the Conservatoire des arts cinématographiques in 1937, where he came first in his class. Two years later, he attended the Conservatoire National d'art dramatique in 1939, where he won second prize in both comedy and tragedy. Reggiani went on to attain great success in the theatre: playing Britannicus in a production by Jean Marais, appearing with Maria Casarès in Camus' *Les Justes* in 1949, directing and playing in *Hamlet* at the Angers festival in 1954, and embodying the tragic hero of Sartre's *Les Sequestrés d'Altona* in 1959. Later, he put his theatrical training and experience to the service of his singing career, which he launched in 1965 with an album of Boris Vian songs.

Reggiani's film career took off during the war, even though as an Italian national – he took French citizenship in 1948 – he was wanted by the Italian authorities for desertion. However, unlike Signoret, his status did not prevent him from working, and his success at the Conservatoire gained him major roles in *Le Voyageur de la Toussaint* (Daquin, 1942) and *Le Carrefour des enfants perdus* (Joannon, 1943), in which he played young hoodlums. After the war, he continued in the 'bad boy' vein playing a collaborator in *Les Portes de la nuit* (Carné, 1946) and a black marketeer in *Manon* (Clouzot, 1949). Reggiani graduated to romantic leads with *Les Amants de Vérone* (Cayatte,

1948), an updating of *Romeo and Juliet*, but he was more frequently cast in supporting roles. He was known for a moody intensity he communicated through his dark, deep-set eyes and his small, wiry frame.[39] At the time of *Casque d'or*, though he may not have been in the same league as Signoret, Reggiani was considered a talented actor with great potential, who embodied a complex masculinity: primarily working class, tough but also vulnerable. In effect, his career may have been affected by the fact that he so often played 'losers' – morally tainted bullies and profiteers whose violent and amoral exterior hid a cowardly core – more in line with Leca than the upright and steadfast Manda. Like Signoret, Reggiani was closely connected with the extremely bleak, noir cinema that is seen as characteristic of the immediate post-war years. Also like Signoret, he valued his privacy, and gave few interviews in the popular film press. The few interviews with him that do exist in *Cinémonde* and *L'Ecran français* from the early 1950s represent him as both a brilliant actor (described by Orson Welles as the best French actor of his generation) and an ordinary family man who viewed his profession as a craft like any other.[40]

While Reggiani and Signoret were building their careers at this time (whatever happened subsequently), Claude Dauphin was already well established in the worlds of cinema and theatre by the time of *Casque d'or*, having appeared in 60 sixty films. Born in 1903, son of the poet Franc-Nohain and brother of the musician, radio and television personality Jean Nohain, Dauphin started out as a set designer in the theatre, before taking to the stage as an actor, becoming known as one of the foremost actors of the 1930s.

Dauphin also appeared in many films at this time, mostly in secondary roles, though he worked with major directors such as Sacha Guitry and Jacques Feyder. His film career took off just before the war with *Entrée des artistes* (Marc Allégret, 1938), appropriately playing a drama student. By the time war broke out, Dauphin was a sought-after romantic lead in films such as *Battement de cœur* (Decoin, 1940, with Danielle Darrieux) and *Félicie Nanteuil* (Marc Allégret, 1942, with Micheline Presle). However, as a member of the Free French Army from 1942, Dauphin's films were banned in Occupied and Vichy France (*Félicie Nanteuil* was not released until 1945). Although he made films in Britain and Hollywood during this time – *The Gentle Sex* (Leslie Howard and Maurice Elvey, 1943), *English without Tears* (Harold French, 1944) and *Salute to France* (Renoir, 1944) – he never regained his position as a vedette in French film after the war. When he died in 1978, he was regarded as a bastion of French theatre, cinema and television thanks to the subtlety and refinement of his performances.[41]

Performance

All three of these performers, especially Signoret and Reggiani, were known for the authenticity of their performances. *Casque d'or*'s realism has already been attributed to its evocation of the ordinary, and this is a key part of performance in the film too. The film consistently emphasises mundane, everyday activities while major events or strong emotions are conveyed with a look, or a very small gesture. This minimalist performance style is often associated with the notion of authenticity because it works against the melodramatic potential of the film – eschewing the repertoire of stock gestures associated with melodrama for a more 'realistic' and sober form of bodily expression. This remains true of Signoret and Reggiani's performances even at the most dramatic moments of the film, as for example, when Marie, desperate because Manda has given himself up to the police, turns for help to Leca, her last hope. The range of emotions from anxiety and a glimmer of hope as she tells him of her problem, to disappointment, fear and disgust as he demands sex in return for a promise of help, is expressed through Signoret's eyes and with a slight hardening of her mouth. The use of alternate close-ups on her and Leca's faces recall the passion she shares with Manda – how different these images of Signoret's tear-stained, profoundly disappointed expression are from those in the previous sequences, when her hair, skin, lips and eyes literally shine with love.

The most famous example, though, of the sobriety of performance comes once again from Marie, as the moment of Manda's execution. Throughout her vigil, her expression contains an acute awareness of what is happening. From the coach ride where her unblinking eyes are picked out by the street lighting that falls on them, to the moment when Manda is brought to the guillotine, her courage does not allow her to look away. All the horror of the moment is expressed with only a slight widening of her eyes, and the quickening of her breathing shown by a slight parting of her lips and movements of her shoulders. The flickering of her eyelids and the slow bowing of her head at the moment the blade falls show more effectively than any hysterical outburst the loss that she feels, as if her eyes can no longer focus and part of herself has been cut away.

Reggiani is equally adept at conveying a great deal with only the slightest gesture or look – an ability highlighted by his minimal dialogue. His joy when Marie comes to find him is conveyed at first with a little smile, more visible in his eyes than on his mouth and Marie returns his look. After she kisses him, his smile is frank and open, crinkling his face and lighting up his eyes. He bestows a similar radiant smile on his old pal Raymond, when they meet up at the *guinguette* after so many years, revealing the depth of the friendship between these two former cellmates. There are no great declarations of love in *Casque d'or* – the one time Marie asks Manda if he loves her (when they are watching the wedding) he does not reply – yet the sincerity of their feelings is all the greater for the understated nature in which it is expressed.

Manda's quiet confidence is shown in the sureness of his movements – his direct gaze expresses moral force, his walk and gestures at work are steady, efficient and craftsmanlike, and he acts decisively when he has to (he knocks Roland out with an effective uppercut, and Raymond is unable to dissuade him from fighting Roland – see Figure 6). This contrasts sharply with the macho posturing of many of the *apaches*, who swagger rather than walk. However, there are other moments in the film that suggest Manda's vulnerability, revealing the complexity of his masculinity. During his first waltz with Marie – the moment of seduction – she looks straight at him, challenging him to resist her. Manda, however, at first bashfully lowers his eyes, only meeting her gaze towards the end of the dance. In this scene, the relative sizes of Signoret and Reggiani are particularly striking. They are approximately the same height, but Signoret, who occupies more of the frame with her long wide skirts, flouncy blouse and extravagant hairstyle, appears physically dominant – an unusual situation for the female star. On the other hand, Reggiani/Manda's posture in the dance, firmly gripping Marie around the waist with his other arm held straight down at his side, in no way speaks of hesitation. However,

Figure 6: Face off at the Ange Gabriel: Raymond is unable to prevent the fight.

by the end of the film, Manda has lost all his force. When he is brought out into the prison courtyard, Reggiani's body is limp, he doesn't move of his own accord – his legs barely walk as he is propelled forward, thrust against the board, roughly strapped down and tilted forward, before the image cuts to the falling blade.

Signoret's performance also evolves throughout the film. She dominates the first part, deliberately provocative, adopting a proud stance worthy of her 'helmet' of golden hair. Marie knows that power can only come from her sexual 'value'. Yet she deliberately antagonises Roland, showing she is not prepared to stand for his bullying. As he grows more and more angry, she remains serene, even after he slaps her. When Leca's errand boys, Billy and Ponsard, track her down at Julie's place, she keeps up the performance, 'exploding' in anger at their bullying tactics, and then laughing about it with the admiring Julie. There is no time for any fetishistic ogling of the semi-clothed star's body – she is physically dominant, pushing them out of the room. And in the following scene at Leca's house she again cuts these bullies down to size. Her body language claims an equal position with Leca in this scene, while the *apaches* are banished to the next room. When they introduce her as 'the object', she looks directly at him, hand on one hip, inviting Leca to share her ironic perspective on their behaviour: 'They're extremely gallant, you know – real gentlemen!' Marie mollifies and flatters Leca in this scene, but her tone of voice and body language is matter of fact and confident. Marie 'plays the game' while making clear that she alone owns her body, proprietorially removing Leca's wandering hand from her breast. Her ironic half-smile as Leca literally kicks Roland out of the room shows a slightly sadistic side (and also recalls a scene in *Dédée d'Anvers*, where Signoret as the otherwise gentle Dédée takes great pleasure in watching a street fight, remarking that men never hurt each other enough). The attitude of Marie in this scene reveals her awareness of her shifting position in terms of power relations, and the necessity to alter her behaviour and perform accordingly. Indeed, when she lets her guard drop and cries in front of Leca, she is repaid by his betrayal, and her attempt to stand up to him is met with violence.

Likewise, Claude Dauphin as Leca offers a multi-layered performance, in this case, of phallic masculinity. As long as his authority is not challenged, he remains jovial. However, his narcissism makes him especially vulnerable, and so when Marie flatters him shamelessly, commenting on his new hairstyle, he responds with a fatuous grin, emphasised in a close-up. Unlike Manda, where what you see is what you get, Leca's appearance hides what lies beneath: the bourgeois wine merchant hides the gangster, the jovial boss hides the violent disciplinarian, the dapper and suave exterior hides the cowardly and treacherous nature within. And Dauphin's wartime activities in the Free French Army lent a further ironic and contemporary resonance to his character's denunciations and black-marketeering.

Dauphin's performance as Leca is overwhelmingly – but also comically – phallic. When he hands Signoret/Marie a knife to cut some cheese, he flicks it open, turning first the blade and then the handle towards her, in a medium shot that shows both his face in the background and the knife in the foreground in sharp focus suggesting his violent and sexual potential (after all, he will rape her later in the film). This is the same knife that will kill Roland, and Marie underlines its phallic properties, examining it approvingly before eating the cheese directly from the blade. As the representative of patriarchal authority, Leca is the character most marked by language. He does not act, he gives orders, or denounces. Language is binding: Marie withholds her response to Leca's 'offer' knowing that an answer either way will seal her fate. And yet, language also reveals Leca's masquerade. His bourgeois pretensions are foiled by his strong Parisian accent and use of slang, which situate him firmly in the '*milieu*'. And at the end of the film, faced with Manda wielding a gun, he is no longer able to speak at all.

If *Casque d'or* makes concessions to the wordy quality tradition, it is in the scenes featuring Leca and the *apaches*, notably when they are sharing out the proceeds of the Crédit Lyonnais robbery and in the scene when Anatole's fate becomes clear. Dudley Andrew has criticised the film for 'helping us out with the plot'.[42] Here, clumsy dialogue and stagey gestures overstate the obvious. Raymond kicks Paul to attract his attention to the safe that Leca is opening, on which all eyes are already trained. In the later scene, upon learning of Anatole's demise, one after another the *apaches* reiterate 'So, did it go okay then?', even pointing to a photograph of Roland Lesaffre as Anatole just in case we had missed this plot development.

It could be argued, though, that by 'hamming up' the *apaches* in this way, Becker gently undermines this generic aspect of the film. Their stylised gestures and rather clichéd repartee ensure that they are not taken too seriously, and that the 'gangster' element acts as a foil to Marie and Manda's love story without rivalling it in the narrative. The fact that the *apaches* only really act in this way when they are in a group (we see Raymond, Paul and Guillaume, for example, behaving quite 'naturally' in other contexts) brings us back to the notion of gender identity – in particular their brand of hierarchical, macho masculinity – as performance. In the next section, we will turn to an examination of the construction of femininity in the film through the character of Marie, in order to assess *Casque d'or*'s feminist credentials.

A feminist film?

Casque d'or has been described by Burch and Sellier as 'truly feminist in the modern sense of the term', offering a *mise-en-scène* of the oppressive effects of patriarchy on both genders.[43] Yet in straightforward narrative terms, we see a woman – a *femme fatale*? – disrupting patriarchal order, leading to the downfall of the man (in this case, two men are killed). Dudley Andrew calls Marie 'the mythical destiny of popular romance, over whom father and son will lose their lives'.[44] And yet, Marie's active position means that she is much more than just a 'myth' of womanhood, in fact offering a challenge to traditional notions of femininity. Before examining how Marie transgresses the boundaries of 'normal' female behaviour, however, we must first consider her situation as a prostitute, which has important contemporary resonances, firstly because of the closing of the brothels in the aftermath of the war, and secondly, as a comment on women's socio-economic position in 1950s France.

Contemporary relevance

Prostitution is not an unusual cinematic subject for this time: Signoret had already played whores in several of her films. Indeed, since before the 1930s the prostitute figure could be said to be a staple of French cinema.[45] Prostitution is also an important part of the 'mythology' of the Belle Epoque and features widely in literary adaptations set in and around this period (*Le Plaisir*, *La Ronde*, *Boule de suif* – Christian-Jaque, 1945). Indeed, Amélie Hélie is a part of this mythology. However, *Casque d'or*'s take on this subject is more complex than just presenting it as a part of the Belle Epoque 'atmosphere' and Marie's situation as an 'object' to be sold between men can be read as a comment on the female condition in post-war France as well as a depiction of turn-of-the-century prostitution.

The turn of the century was a transitional moment for prostitution in France, and in Paris especially, entailing the decline of the closely regulated *maisons closes* and the rise of the *fille insoumise*, or the 'independent' prostitute.[46] ('Independent' here refers to their unregulated status: they were just as likely to be controlled by a pimp as other prostitutes.) It is unsurprising, then, that at this time there was an increased fear of disease, since these women were not subject to the health checks carried out on brothel inmates. As a result, any *fille insoumise* who came to the attention of the authorities was registered and from then on subject to state controls.[47] Amélie Hélie worked mainly as a '*fille en carte*' – registered but not tied to a particular brothel, under the control of a *souteneur* (pimp).

In the 1900s, the main discourses on prostitution focused on disease, and the need for regulation as a way of protecting the bourgeoisie from infection. By 1952, though, there had been a dramatic shift towards the question of moral purity. At the Liberation, brothels (highly regulated and sanitised) were denounced as hotbeds of collaboration and profiteering. Many inmates had been accused of 'collaboration horizontale' and publically shorn. While it is true that some women and brothel-keepers had made a handsome profit under the Occupation, not all prostitutes entered into the way of collaboration. Some had been punished severely by German/Vichy authorities for deliberately spreading disease among the Germans.[48] Nonetheless, as part of a raft of purges, the *loi Marthe Richard* was passed in April 1946, outlawing brothels. The result, of course, was not the disappearance of prostitution, but, paradoxically, its increased visibility in a deregulated form, since those women who did not go abroad (to North Africa, for example, where brothels were still legal) instead began to ply their trade on the street.[49]

So *Casque d'or*'s depiction of unregulated prostitution controlled by pimps and gangsters refers to a very contemporary debate. Hayward has argued that Signoret's roles as prostitute 'or woman on the make' offer a consistent image of women who control their own bodies, as objects of economic exchange and as desiring subjects. In the rare cases when her character is under the thumb of a pimp (*Dédée d'Anvers* and *Casque d'or*), he is eliminated during the course of the narrative.[50] For Hayward, there is a possible Marxist reading of these films that allows them to be read 'against the grain' as offering images of women who regulate their own sexuality outside of patriarchal structures. Arguably, though, a 'reading against the grain' of these films is made possible not so much by the fact that Signoret's character sells her own labour, as because her desire is consistently privileged by both narrative and *mise-en-scène*, via Signoret's performances and the gaze. She is therefore presented as a fully-fledged subject who just happens to be a prostitute. For example, in *Dédée d'Anvers*, the opening sequence shows Dédée strolling through the port of Antwerp and setting eyes on Francesco (Marcel Pagliero), the sailor with whom she will experience passionate love. Their exchange of desiring looks is initiated by Dédée. Likewise in *Casque d'or*, Marie and Manda's reciprocal passion is set up in the first sequence. In both cases, Signoret's character's desire is given a dominant narrative position as a force that disrupts the power relations to which she is subject, and as the means by which her characters attempt to liberate themselves from patriarchal control.

It is instructive to compare Signoret's prostitutes in these films with Martine Carol's eponymous Nana, in Christian-Jaque's 1955 film. Nana is utterly defined by her condition: she relies completely on men for the material comforts with which she surrounds herself, but ruins each suitor in turn. She is shown in the exercise of her profession, constantly on display. Her relationships with other women are defined through rivalry or financial exchange. Nana's own desire is entirely subordinated to necessity, mostly financial. Indeed, Nana becomes the stake of a bet between Muffat and Vendeuvres, a bet which both men lose, but which she will not survive either. In any case, Nana could never be free of her condition, since all she ever wishes for is to replace one protector with another, and all her relationships are based on manipulation and profit.

Through the opposition of the debauched Nana and Muffat's devout wife (Elisa Cegani), Christian-Jaque's film upholds post-war discourses that presented prostitution as a menace to bourgeois morality: it is not just Muffat's marriage that is destroyed but also the engagement of his daughter and her prospects, while his wife is 'driven' to adultery. And, the collapse of the bank owned by another suitor, Steiner (Noël Roquevert), brought about by Nana's profligacy, is an assault on the ruling classes, threatening the stability of the nation.[51] In Zola's novel, the final image of Nana is of a hideous, rotting corpse, which represents the infectious dangers of disease associated with prostitution. Christian-Jaque's Nana, however, is strangled by Muffat in a jealous rage, punished by the very classes she threatened, and in this way, she is contained, her beauty preserved in the film's final images of a glassy-eyed, doll-like Martine Carol.

Casque d'or, on the other hand, thanks to Marie's refusal to submit to her situation – we never see her taking money, or expressing any interest in material wealth – highlights the hypocrisy of the double standard that denies the parallels between the sexual economies of marriage and prostitution.[52] In 1950s France married women could be prevented from working by their husbands, and many women worked unpaid in family businesses such as farms or shops. In short, the vast majority of women were financially and legally dependent on men. This question of female dependence, then, extends far beyond the realm of prostitution, and this is why Marie's resistance of the commodification of her body has such an important contemporary significance.[53]

A 'real' woman

Marie, then, is not solely defined as a prostitute – she is a complex and evolving character. She is undeniably sexual: and while her desire is crucial in defining her as a subject in her own right (and not a mere object desired by various men), the form of this desire and the way she expresses it shifts throughout the film from her almost aggressive seduction of Manda to her determination to save him. Neither is Marie solely defined in terms of her relationships with men: she is admired by her fellow prostitutes and enjoys a close friendship with Julie. She is both a public object of display and desire (her job) and a woman with her own private desires. Though she plays up to her public role when necessary, Marie is also elusive, refusing to fully occupy the space of gangster's moll. In keeping with her public persona, she acts the 'garce' in the first part of the film, provoking Roland and leading Manda on, instigating the fight at the Ange Gabriel and then wordlessly walking away from Manda after he has killed Roland, leaving him to Leca's taunts. Yet even before she sets up Manda's escape to the countryside there are clues to her 'private' desires. The moment she steals with Manda at the *guinguette* when they say goodbye gives her the courage to withstand Roland's bullying. Her fury when she discovers Manda's attachment to Léonie is what leads her to react so dismissively when he appears at the Ange Gabriel to 'take her away'. Her involuntary shudder as Leca's hand lingers on her bare shoulder in the same sequence, and her desperation to escape with Julie so she doesn't have to go home with him, hint that Leca's assumption of victory over Manda is premature. Indeed, when they are gathered outside the Ange Gabriel looking in at Roland's corpse, she betrays her concern for Manda to Leca by worriedly asking Raymond if he escaped. Yet Marie is not without fault: she enjoys seeing others humiliated and she can be violent – Manda has to restrain her from attacking Léonie (see Figure 7). In her desperation to save Manda she encourages him to forget about Raymond. This lends a certain ambiguity to her actions: is she trying to save Manda, or preserve her own happiness? The selflessness of Marie's love only becomes clear in the final sequence when she watches over Manda to the end, even though he doesn't know she is there.

It is this complexity of her characterisation that enables Marie to transcend the label of 'garce'. And indeed, the visual treatment of her character reinforces her centrality to the narrative through her frequent positioning in the middle of the frame, with other characters arranged around her (see Figure 5). It is also the case that Marie and Manda's love is represented as evolving from seduction to passion to quasi-conjugal devotion: demonstrated during their 'honeymoon' in Joinville, and in the final part of the film, which shows that her commitment to Manda is for worse as well as for better. This is why Marie is more than just an expression of a traditional myth of woman-hood: her character exposes femininity as a construction, just as the macho posturings of Leca and his gang make a mockery of certain masculine traits. In this way (as well as in the casting of the slight Reggiani and the majestic

Signoret) Becker's film both acknowledges and subverts traditional representations of masculinity as active and femininity as passive. Marie shows the necessary multiplicity of gender identity, constantly redefined according to circumstances, and her shifting position within the relations of power. This evolution in Marie's position can be seen clearly in the dynamics of the gaze in *Casque d'or*.

The active gaze

Marie first lays eyes on Manda at the *guinguette* in the opening sequence, when she is dancing with Roland. Manda is instantly seduced, he returns her gaze, following the couple's progress around the room as they waltz. In reviewing *Casque d'or* for the (extremely conservative) weekly magazine *Noir et Blanc*, Hervé Lauwick wrote:

> [Signoret] executes a little waltz in front of Serge Reggiani without losing sight of him…at each moment, following the orders of the director, her head is turned towards Serge Reggiani. It's the most astounding and vertiginous thing we've seen in 1952…an actress like Simone Signoret…doesn't need to stare at a man like that to show her intentions.[54]

This passage highlights the disturbing qualities of her gaze: although Lauwick is right when he reminds us that Signoret is 'following the orders of her director', his comment has the effect of denying (or at least diluting) the strong impression of her character's agency conveyed by Signoret's

Figure 7: Marie, taunted by Léonie, is held back by Manda.

performance and the *mise-en-scène*, before suggesting that there are more appropriate (and discreet) ways for expressing female desire (though without detailing what these might be). This raises the question of why her look is so troubling. One answer can be offered by a closer look at this sequence, which reveals that the dynamics of seduction are constantly shifting, with both Manda and Marie occupying what might traditionally be seen as masculine and feminine positions.

When Marie spots Manda, we see the quality of her look change, from one of friendly greeting (to Raymond) to one of sexual interest – a traditionally masculine position. Her eyes remain fixed on Manda throughout her dance with Roland, her look returned by the carpenter. Marie's look challenges: Manda's is intrigued. When the dance is over, Marie walks away, turning to make sure Manda's eyes remain on her, thus positioning herself as the now feminine object of his look. Raymond persuades Manda to meet his friends, and as they approach the group, there is a tracking shot from Manda's point of view, moving forward into the group and turning towards the left, excluding Roland from the frame while positioning Marie towards the centre. Their eyes remain fixed on each other as she again adopts the active role, asking him to dance. We have seen how, during their dance, Manda at first avoids Marie's frank gaze, but then returns it, leading the dance with increasing confidence and leaving her in a spin at the end. Marie's gaze may have seduced Manda, but he returns it fully throughout this scene, and the final close-ups – first of Marie, then Manda – when she comes to say goodbye, arguably show their equality in terms of the expression of their desire. The use of close-up and medium close-ups privilege the face as the site of desiring looks: in particular the eyes and the smile are eroticised. But the other's body is not objectified or fetishised – the destination of the look is the site of the returning look, suggesting that *Casque d'or* offers a rare *mise-en-scène* of heterosexual desire as mutual.

Much of feminist film theory has concentrated on the dynamics of the gaze, both within a film's diegesis and in relation to spectators, as indicative of the way that classical narrative cinema positions women as passive objects and men as active subjects. Laura Mulvey's well-known 1975 article 'Visual pleasure and narrative cinema' argues that women occupy either the position of enigma to be investigated or that of fetish to be venerated.[55] Feminist theory has pursued the vexed questions of the representation of femininity and the positioning of the female spectator, and in many cases, it is argued that women are required to read films 'against the grain' in order to be able to identify with female characters.[56] In *Casque d'or*, though, Marie's active gaze invites a much more direct identification from spectators, yet she does not as a result occupy a 'masculine' position. In this way, *Casque d'or* challenges the equation of masculinity with activity and femininity with passivity, showing that it is necessary for both men and women to shift between these two positions.

This constantly shifting dynamic between active bearer of the gaze and passive object of the look is again demonstrated in a later scene. Manda is asleep on the riverbank, when Marie comes into view in her boat. As she rows towards him, we share her point of view of the sleeping fugitive. In a reversal of the Sleeping Beauty fairy tale, Marie first teases her lover and then awakens him with a kiss (see Figure 3). As Manda awakens, we cut to a close-up of Marie looking down with the sun behind her, her eyes full of love and her golden hair shimmering. There follows a fade to black – the next shot shows Manda in bed gazing down on Marie's sleeping form, thus maintaining a balance in their relationship. So while *Casque d'or* offers a rare representation of female desire, it also recognises that there is little point in being a desiring subject if one is not desired in return (which is Leca's fate). Thus the look implies seduction as well as desire and demands a returning look.

The gaze in *Casque d'or* is not purely one of desire. Manda and Raymond's friendship is communicated not by words, but through their exchange of looks, for example, when Manda gives himself up to clear Raymond. And in the final sequence, Marie looks with horror at her lover's execution – to look away would constitute a betrayal. The gaze confers subjectivity which implies responsibility as well as desire – responsibility Marie assumes with her vigil. The active look is evidence of the Marie's evolution, from a proud woman whose actions are directed towards herself and improving her own situation, to committed and loyal lover who sacrifices herself for her partner, and even when she is unable to save him, shows solidarity with him in his final, terrible moments.

Georges Sadoul saw *Casque d'or* as lacking in substance and yet as representing the apotheosis of Becker's style: meticulous attention to detail in the depiction of the characters and their environment, elegant mastery of camerawork and editing, and spot-on direction of his actors.[57] However, a close analysis of the film has demonstrated that Becker's 'style' is inseparable from the substance of his film. All Becker's films are concerned with the everyday – his characters brought to life through detailed observation and re-creation of ordinary gestures. *Casque d'or* is remarkable in taking a range of stock characters – the gang leader, the moll, and the honest worker, not to mention the loyal pal and the corrupt policeman – and 'bringing them to life'. The stylistic elements discussed here – narrative structure, with its emphasis on different chronotopes associated with particular characters, the cause–effect chain that links the sequences according to the characters' desires, the *mise-en-scène* and the editing, and the use of stars – are all placed at the service of Becker's characters: of Marie and Manda and those they encounter. And here is where the true substance of *Casque d'or* lies: in the creation of believable, memorable characters, who transcend stereotypes in order to challenge contemporary expectations regarding relations between men and women – even definitions of masculinity and femininity. Unfortunately, at the time, this achievement was not recognised, and the film's reception in France was far from triumphant. The next part will go on to examine this reception in more detail, looking at the reasons why it took so long for *Casque d'or* to be regarded as a classic of French cinema.

Notes

1   'Chronotope' literally means 'time-space', and emphasises the inseparability of these two concepts in a narrative. See Bakhtin, Mikhail, 'Forms of time and of the chronotope in the novel', in *The Dialogic Imagination: Four essays*, trans. Caryl Emerson and Michael Holquist (Austin: University of Texas Press, 1981), pp. 84–258.

2   Hayward: *Simone Signoret*, pp. 31–33.

3   Andrew: '*Casque d'or, casquettes*', p. 115.

4   Rivette and Truffaut: 'Entretien avec Jacques Becker', p. 14.

5   Tarnowski, Jean-Louis, *Essais d'esthétique et de philosophie du cinéma: pour une théorie générale de l'art cinématographique*, unpublished doctoral thesis, Université de Paris I (Lille: A.R.N.T., 1987), p. 144.

6   Andrew: '*Casque d'or, casquettes*', p. 116.

7   Vincendeau, Ginette, 'Daddy's girls: Oedipal narratives in 1930s French films', *Iris* 8 (1988), pp. 70–81, p. 79.

8   Examples include *Manon* (Clouzot, 1949), *Les Miracles n'ont lieu qu'une fois* (Yves Allégret, 1951), *La Vérité sur Bébé Donge* (Decoin, 1952), *Lola Montès* (Ophüls, 1955).

9   Leahy, Sarah, '"Neither charm nor sex appeal ... " Just what is the appeal of Simone Signoret?', *Studies in French Cinema* 4.1 (2004), pp. 29–40, pp. 35–36.

10 Rivette and Truffaut: 'Entretien avec Jacques Becker', p. 4.

11 See, for example: Bazin, André, 'An aesthetic of reality: Cinematic realism and the Italian school of the liberation', in *What is Cinema?* vol. 2, trans. by Hugh Gray (Berkeley, Los Angeles, London: University of California Press, 1971), pp. 16–40; Bondanella, Peter, *Italian Cinema: From neorealism to the present* (New York: Frederick Ungar, 1983); Overby, David (ed.), *Springtime in Italy: A reader on neo-realism* (London: Talismann, 1978); Sorlin, Pierre, *Italian National Cinema* (London and New York: Routledge, 1996).

12 See Bazin, André, '*Antoine et Antoinette*', *Le Parisien libéré*, 21 September 1947, cited in Naumann: *Jacques Becker*, p. 158; Bazin, André, '*La Rue de l'Estrapade*', *Observateur d'aujourd'hui*, 14 May 1953, cited in Naumann: Jacques Becker, pp. 170–171; Néry, Jean, '*Rue de l'Estrapade*', *Franc-Tireur*, 21 April 1953; and Sadoul: 'Puissance de la sobriété'.

13   Bazin: 'An aesthetic of reality', p. 26.

14   Bazin: 'An aesthetic of reality', p. 28. Bazin actually discusses deep focus in relation to *Citizen Kane*.

15   See Crisp: *The Classic French Cinema*, pp. 400–402; Vincendeau, Ginette, 'The art of spectacle: The aesthetics of classical French cinema', in Michael Temple and Michael Witt (eds), *The French Cinema Book* (London: BFI, 2004), pp. 137–152, p. 145.

16   Vincendeau: 'The art of spectacle', p. 145.

17   Crisp: *The Classic French Cinema*, p. 402.

18   Alain Resnais, 'Le Bonheur au quotidien', in Claude Beylie and Freddy Buache (eds), *Jacques Becker* (Locarno: Editions du Festival de Locarno, 1991), p. 229.

19   Bazin, 'An aesthetic of reality', p. 21.

20   Most of Becker's films were shot partly on location and partly in studios, though *Edouard et Caroline* was filmed entirely in a studio. See also Naumann: *Jacques Becker*, pp. 28–29.

21   Rendu, Marc-Ambroise, 'La Maison de *Casque d'or* sera conservée', *Le Monde*, 21 October 1992.

22   Naumann: *Jacques Becker*, p. 54.

23   Their first kiss also takes place outside, on a waste ground in Belleville.

24   Signoret, *La Nostalgie…*, p. 116.

25   Entwistle, Joanne, 'The dressed body', in Joanne Entwistle and Elizabeth Wilson (eds), *Body Dressing* (Oxford and New York: Berg, 2001), pp. 33–58, p. 37.

26   Laver, James, *Modesty in Dress*, 1969, p. 173; cited in Bruzzi, Stella, *Undressing Cinema: Clothing and identity in the movies* (London and New York: Routledge, 1997), p. 41.

27   Malliarakis, Nikita, *Mayo: Un peintre et le cinéma* (Paris: L'Harmattan, 2002), p. 71.

28   Hayward, Susan, 'Signoret's star persona and redressing the costume cinema: Jacques Becker's *Casque d'or* (1952)', *Studies in French Cinema* 4.1 (2004), pp. 15–28, p. 26.

29   Hayward: 'Signoret's star persona', p. 17.

30   Becker, Jacques, '*Casque d'or*', *L'Avant-scène cinéma* 43 (December 1964), pp. 7–60, p. 40.

31   Truffaut, François, 'De vraies moustaches', *L'Avant-scène cinéma* 43 (December 1964), p. 6.

32   Varennes: 'Gazette des tribunaux', p. 4.

33   Bruzzi: *Undressing Cinema*, p. 75.

34   Signoret: *La Nostalgie…*, p. 127.

35   Vincendeau: *Stars and Stardom in French Cinema*, pp. viii–ix.

36   See David: *Simone Signoret*, p. 110; Anderson, Katherine, 'A sign of her times: the young Simone Signoret as star', unpublished MA essay, University of Warwick 1998, pp. 11–13; Hayward, Susan, 'Simone Signoret 1921–1985: The star as sign – The sign As scar', in Diana Knight and Judith Still (eds), *Women and Representation* (London: WIF, 1995), pp. 57–74, p. 59.

37   Sadoul: 'Puissance de la sobriété'.

38   Signoret, *La Nostalgie…*, p. 118.

39   See, for example, Anon., 'Serge Reggiani', *Unifrance Film*, no date (BFI microjacket); Anon., 'Serge Reggiani', *The Times*, 28 July 2004, p. 53; Kirkup, James, 'Serge Reggiani: popular actor turned singer', *Independent*, 26 July 2004, p. 34. NB: Page numbers are not available for some articles found in the BFI holdings of press cuttings. They will be given when possible.

40 Beaume, Georges, 'Serge Reggiani, sera un jour le successeur de Pierre Fresnay', *Cinémonde*, 17 October 1952, pp. 7–9; Bergut, Bob, 'Comment faire la conquête morale de Serge Reggiani', *L'Ecran français* no. 271, 18 September 1950, pp. 4–5.

41 Schidlow, Joshka, 'Claude Dauphin', *Télérama* no. 1507, 2 December 1978, p. 11.

42 Andrew: '*Casque d'or, casquettes*', p. 120.

43 Burch and Sellier: *La Drôle de guerre des sexes*, p. 18.

44 Andrew: '*Casque d'or, casquettes*', p. 114.

45 For example, *Nana* (Renoir, 1925) starring Catherine Hessling; *Pépé le Moko* (Duvivier, 1936) and *Gueule d'amour* (Grémillon, 1937) starring Mireille Balin; *L'Hôtel du nord* (Carné, 1938) with Arletty; *Macadam* (Blistène, 1946), *Dédée d'Anvers* (Allégret, 1948) starring Signoret. Even when the woman is not actually paid for sex, she is frequently sent by her 'pimp' to seduce an 'innocent' man for financial gain. See for example *La Chienne* (Renoir, 1931) with Janie Marèse and *Panique* (Duvivier, 1946) with Viviane Romance. And in many films, 'ordinary' women are shown to have been prostitutes (Florelle/Valentine, in *Le Crime de Monsieur Lange*, Renoir, 1936) or are mistaken for one (Michèle Morgan/Nelly in *Quai des brumes*, Carné, 1938).

46 Corbin: *Women for Hire*, p. 37. On this subject, see also McMillan, James F., *Housewife or Harlot: The place of women in French society 1870–1940* (Brighton: Harvester Press, 1981) and McMillan, James F., *France and Women 1789–1914: Gender, Society and politics* (London and New York: Routledge, 2000).

47 Corbin: *Women for Hire*, p. 86, p. 122 and pp. 132–133.

48 Corbin: *Women for Hire*, p. 346.

49 Van Haecht, Anne, *La Prostituée: Statut et image* (Brussels: Editions de l'Université de Bruxelles, 1973), p. 65. Signoret's earlier role in *Dédée d'Anvers* refers to the expatriation of French prostitutes after the war.

50 Hayward: *Simone Signoret*, pp. 37–38.

51 This is an interesting reversal of the position in Christian-Jaque's earlier film, *Boule de suif* (1945), starring Micheline Presle, in which the bourgeoisie is represented as corrupt, venal and hypocritical, while the prostitute is left to save the nation.

52 Fortescue, W., *The Third Republic in France 1870–1940: Conflicts and continuities* (London and New York: Routledge, 2000), p. 97. See also Duchen, Claire, 'Occupation housewife: The domestic ideal in 1950s France', *French Cultural Studies*, 2.1/4 (1991), pp. 1–11.

53 See Duchen: *Women's Rights and Women's Lives*, p. 129 and p. 146, and Lehmann: *Le Rôle de la femme française*, p. 7.

54 Lauwick, Hervé, '*Casque d'or*', *Noir et Blanc*, 30 April 1952, p. 17.

55 Mulvey, Laura, 'Visual pleasure and narrative cinema', in *Visual and Other Pleasures* (London: Macmillan, 1989), pp. 14–26.

56 Further influential work in this area includes Doane, Mary Ann, *Femmes Fatales: Feminism, Film Theory and Psychoanalysis* (New York and London: Routledge, 1991) and Gledhill, Christine, 'Pleasurable Negotiations', in Sue Thornham (ed.), *Feminist Film Theory: A Reader* (Edinburgh: Edinburgh University Press, 1999), pp. 166–179.

57 Sadoul: 'Puissance de la sobriété'.

3   Reception at home
and abroad

French and British views

Casque d'or had its world premiere in Brussels in April 1952. In *La Nostalgie n'est plus ce qu'elle était*, Simone Signoret describes the experience of attending this opening night:

> I asked, 'Don't you like it?' They sorrowfully shook their heads. Only one grasped the mettle and said, 'It's weak, it's very weak.' *Casque d'or*, presented in a gala première in Brussels, only remained on the programme for four days. And, for once, Paris followed Brussels, who had set the trend. After *Casque d'or*, Serge went five years without making another film.[1]

However, the film's lack of domestic success was not matched in its international career, as Signoret continues:

> Then rumours began to arrive from abroad. In London, *Golden Mary* was greeted as a masterpiece, in Rome, *Casco d'oro* was making a fortune, in Berlin, the same thing. Finally, we were being recognized. We weren't the victims of a collective miscalculation. We really and truly had made a beautiful film.

It is true that *Casque d'or* was not very well received by French critics or public. This was a time when audience figures for French films were soaring – the most successful French film of the year, *Le Petit monde de Don Camillo* (Julien Duvivier), attracted almost 12.8 million spectators.[2] And in this one year, there were a further six French films with over 3 million spectators: *Violettes Impériales* (Pottier, 8.1 million), *Fanfan la tulipe* (Christian-Jaque, 6.7 million), *Jeux interdits* (Clément, 4.9 million), *Le Fruit défendu* (Verneuil, 4 million), *Belles de nuit* (Clair, 3.5 million) and *Nous sommes tous des assassins* (Cayatte, 3 million). *Casque d'or* sold the relatively disappointing figure of

1.9 million tickets in France, though for a medium-budget film, this is not quite the flop Signoret seems to suggest. Unfortunately, box office figures are not available for *Casque d'or*'s international career. Press reviews, however, offer an invaluable insight into the domestic and international reception of the film. As Signoret points out, British reviewers championed the film and so this section will offer a comparison of the British and French reviews of *Casque d'or* at the time of its release in each country (April 1952 in France and September of the same year in Britain).

France

This section will offer a general overview of contemporary critical opinion. Among reviews examined are two entirely positive (Lang and Boussinot), and two entirely negative (Frank, who nonetheless spares the actors, and Doniol-Valcroze). The remainder (Lauwick, Quéval, Magnan, Sadoul) are nuanced, finding reasons to praise the film but with important reservations. While this is hardly the critical slating described by Signoret and others, French reviews are much less enthusiastic than British ones, as we shall see. What is of particular interest here is what these reviews reveal in terms of critics' concerns, through the elements of the film singled out for praise or censure.

French reviews focus on two main areas of the film: subject matter and aesthetics. The overwhelming complaint is about the subject itself, seen as clichéd and unworthy of the talent involved.[3] The period setting is seen as a mistake for Becker, celebrated for his portraits of contemporary society (indeed, this is Doniol-Valcroze's principal objection). Complaints of vulgarity refer to the dialogue – regularly singled out as the weakest point of the film because of its obvious simplicity, swearing and slang – but also, rather strangely given Becker's reputation for elegance and modesty (*pudeur*), to the visual references to bodily functions (Mère Adèle emptying her slop pails, the coach driver urinating against the wall).[4] The film is also criticised as excessively violent in terms of the number of slaps exchanged between characters as well as murders and the execution, though Leca's sexual violence is not mentioned.[5] For many, the film lacks subtlety, and the frank expression of female sexual desire is both unnecessary and undesirable.[6] Reviewers emphasise the melodramatic or sensational, as did the French censorship body, which demanded cuts in the execution scene, until Becker persuaded them to restore the sequence.[7] This suggests that the overall consensus is that the film lacks credibility and yet there is consistent praise for the authenticity of the period reconstruction as well as the quality of acting of the entire cast. The virtuoso camera work and the rhythm and finesse of the editing are also praised.[8] However, there are recurring stylistic criticisms. One of these refers to the lack of unity of the film in terms of tone and genre – seen by Henri Magnan of *Le Monde* and Jean Quéval of *Radio-Cinéma-Télévision* as confusing for viewers who do not know whether they are watching a realist drama or a parodic period crime film.[9] Yet for André Lang, the 'mix of genres' is a positive sign of Becker's non-conformism, even if it could perplex 'less discerning' viewers.[10] Indeed, a closer examination of the discussion of style reveals a lack of consensus among critics regarding *Casque d'or*. Magnan complains about the over-insistence on the Belle Époque setting, which he claims renders each image an 'ephemeral vignette', interesting in themselves but not forming a dramatic whole. On the other hand, Jacques Doniol-Valcroze writing in *France-Observateur* acknowledges Becker's skill in avoiding the fussy, '*faux* 1900' style of *Gigi* or *Le Plaisir*, and in presenting a more realistic image of turn-of-the-century Paris, but he simultaneously suggests that a more stylised form would have better suited the 'timeless' nature of the tragedy. Bazin laments the contradiction between the realism of the *mise-en-scène* and the invention of the story, as a betrayal of Becker's realist intentions, while for Georges Charensol, the invented story is what maintains the spectators' interest. And to bring yet another perspective, Quéval admires Becker's ability to maintain a balance between realism and parody.[11]

This was not, then, the uniform critical thrashing that is part of the 'myth' of *Casque d'or*. Rather, the 'new Becker' did not live up to critics' expectations, seen as betraying his realist 'vocation' (in fact, imposed by these same critics on the basis of his earlier films) with the film's period setting, its 'flimsy' plot, and its depiction of the 'picturesque' criminal classes. It would appear, though, that these expectations are specifically French. Let us turn to the British press coverage in order to gain an international perspective.

Britain

Casque d'or appeared quite rapidly on British screens, only a few months after its French release, and was was shown at only one cinema in London compared with four in Paris. Twenty reviews have been examined, of which twelve offer almost exclusively positive comments on the film.[12] There are five mixed reviews where the subject matter is seen as problematic,[13] and a further three negative reviews, though none that are as dismissive as the more critical French reviews.[14] There is, then, a marked difference between British and French opinion of the film overall.

Casque d'or was released in Britain in the same week as Yves Allégret's film *Dédée d'Anvers*, which had appeared on French screens in 1948. Both films featured Simone Signoret as a prostitute who finds love and a chance to escape her way of life, only for her to lose her lover at the end of the film (in *Dédée*, he is shot in the back by her cowardly pimp). While in some ways this highlighted the more formulaic aspects of the films (the setting in the *milieu*, the kind-hearted prostitute, the vicious and vain pimp), in fact many reviews focus on the nuanced performances of Signoret and the skill of the directors in lifting the films out of cliché. The parallel trajectories of the heroines and the similar marginal, underworld settings of the films (Belle Époque Belleville and the docks of post-war Antwerp) feature in several reviews.[15] One further element that is present in the British reviews is a discussion of the film's Frenchness – suggesting that while it is permissible for an 'exotic' French film to broach certain subjects and to show certain images, this would not be acceptable in a British film.[16] *Casque d'or* is generally seen as treating an adult theme in an uncompromising yet entertaining way. There are some dissenters, notably Winnington, writing in the *News Chronicle*, and the *Daily Worker* critic, who, like some more left-wing French critics, suspect that such talent is rather wasted on this subject matter.

Casque d'or is thus seen as a straightforward period drama – there is no discussion of any possible contemporary relevance. This is also true in the French reviews, which recall 'popular' legends of the Belle Époque: the songs of Aristide Bruant, the notorious anarchist Bonnot and his gang, and of course the story of the *apaches* and Amélie Hélie. British reviewers, on the other hand, invoke Renoir, Monet and especially Toulouse-Lautrec as well as Maupassant and Daudet – references which, once again, firmly anchor the film in the Belle Époque, but also imply a certain literary or artistic stylisation that is not perceived in France. French reviews do not make so many painterly references, perhaps more familiar with the type of illustrated journalism from the period that Becker claimed as his principal source. In the British context, only Gavin Lambert, in the *Evening Standard*, refers to the 'directness' of Becker's reconstruction of the past as being without 'overt visual reference to Lautrec or Renoir', and as 'making the past as naturally, continuously alive as the present'.[17] For Lambert this is one of the chief accomplishments of the film along with its focus on human relationships. The actors, especially Signoret, are highly acclaimed, though some critics (Winnington in the *News Chronicle* and *The Times*' critic) remain unconvinced by Reggiani's performance as Manda, the one seeing him as carried by Signoret, the other as overwhelmed by her. Dilys Powell, writing in the *Sunday Times*, enjoys the understatedness of the acting, and of the film generally. She places Marie's evolution at the heart of the film, but still sees her as a *femme fatale*: 'The girl with the golden hair softens after her first casual summons to the stranger, and at the core of the film is her transformation as she realises that she has destroyed the man with whom she is in love.[18] Character development is seen as much more important in the British reviews than in the French ones and they refer to Manda and Marie's relationship as evolving from physical passion to deep love. In general terms, the acting and direction are highly praised, seen as preventing this rather 'squalid' tale from 'descending' irrevocably into melodrama.

Another difference is the British critics' praise of a flowing, sensuous film. In the country of Shakespeare, there are no complaints about any lack of unity of genre or tone: rather, the lighter moments of the film are seen as leaving a lasting impression of beauty and as rendering the tragic *dénouement* more poignant, or, as Powell puts it: 'Perhaps the contrast between the confident flesh and the overtaking tragedy is what gives the tale its especial mood of grief.'[19]

Lindsay Anderson, writing in *Sight and Sound*, highlights these contrasting moods of the film in terms of Becker's influences: the painter Renoir for the 'happier phases of the story' and Eugène Sue for the 'narrative of plotting and intrigue'.[20] For Anderson, Becker's realism is closely connected to his actors' performances – especially Signoret and Reggiani – and this sobriety is what 'lifts' the film from melodrama into the realm of tragedy. Anderson compares *Casque d'or* with the Carné–Prévert masterpieces of the 1930s finding it more mature, replacing fate with human responsibility. His only criticism is that the 'directness and simplicity' of the love story between Marie and Manda is rather lost in the gangster plot, which he finds confused, due to what he sees as Leca's shallowness. As we shall see, Anderson's comments on the film would eventually influence those of French critics, notably Bazin, who radically revised his opinion of *Casque d'or* in 1955.[21]

In Britain, then, *Casque d'or* was warmly received as the latest offering from a familiar director (*Goupi Mains Rouges, Antoine et Antoinette* and *Edouard et Caroline* had all been released in Britain), with a star who was also known to the British public for her work in French films (*Manèges* and *La Ronde*) but also thanks to her starring role in a British war film: *Against the Wind* (Crichton, 1948). Its 'honest' representation of sexuality and its tough attitude towards underworld violence conform to expectations of 'Continental' films as offering the British public X-certificate films dealing with 'adult' subjects. And while there may be a general air of moral disapproval regarding these themes (themes that would not be broached in such a frank way by British cinema until the New Wave of the late 1950s, when Signoret was to bring her forthright sensuality and desiring femininity to the part of Alice Aisgill in *Room at the Top*, Clayton, 1959), there is also a recognition that the 'humanity' of Becker's film transcends stereotype.

Lindsay Anderson was to define the *Casque d'or* debate in national terms in his letter to the *Cahiers du cinéma* one year later, on the occasion of the release of Becker's next film, *Rue de l'Estrapade*:

> The differences that exist between countries in matters of taste are a commonplace when it comes to art. [...] For example, our admiration for *Casque d'or* astonishes you. But one must stick to one's guns: I am right and you are wrong.[22]

History would seem to be on Anderson's side, and to suggest that French critics – even the 'Young Turks' who challenged the politically motivated tradition of French film criticism with their writing in journals such as the *Cahiers du cinéma* – failed to recognise the aesthetic daring of *Casque d'or*. Nonetheless, the film was seen as important enough to provoke some debate, both in *Cahiers du cinéma* and in *Les Lettres françaises*. Let us now move on to a consideration of these debates as a way of shedding further light on the reasons for the disparity between the French and British reception of the film.

The *Casque d'or* debate: *Les Lettres françaises* and *Les Cahiers du cinéma*

Undoubtedly, the two most influential film critics in France in 1952 were André Bazin and Georges Sadoul. Both Bazin and Sadoul became engaged in debates regarding *Casque d'or*, and both came to revise their initial opinions of the film, Sadoul for the worse and Bazin for the better. This section will take their articles as a starting point to look at the critical debates surrounding the film that took place among the Communist critics of *L'Ecran français* and *Les Lettres françaises* (including Sadoul), and among those critics associated with *Les Cahiers du cinéma*, the home of François Truffaut, Jean-Luc Godard, Jacques Rivette and other *enfants terribles* of film criticism, more associated with the 'politique des auteurs'. These debates are extremely revealing not just about *Casque d'or*, but also about some dominant concerns of writing on French cinema at this time. Valérie Vignaux suggests that *Casque d'or* was somehow the victim of these debates, falling into the ideological gulf that separated the *Cahiers du cinéma* and the *Lettres françaises*, and in particular Bazin and Sadoul.[23]

Colin Crisp identifies four main critical discourses that dominated writing on French film in the classical period, especially after the war: firstly, the discourse of art (and of the *auteur*), most closely associated with *Cahiers du cinéma*; secondly, the moral discourse, expounded especially by the Catholic Church; thirdly, the discourse of pleasure, which flourished in the popular film magazines; and finally, the discourse of the real, which encompassed many different debates, including that of social realism, which dominated in left-wing publications that sought to define what a true cinema of the people would be.[24] However, as Crisp points out, it is too simple to pigeonhole these approaches to particular publications. In fact, 'serious' criticism in France since the 1920s had been characterised by 'the well-known romantic discourse of the author as creative artist', and even in the post-war period, this was not confined to *Cahiers du cinéma*, but appeared also in the left-wing *Ecran français* and *Positif*.[25] Similarly, the discourse of the real is not confined to social realist concerns, as we see when we consider Bazin's influential writings on the relationship between cinema and what it portrays.[26] The key debates that will concern us here relate to realism and art. Once again, this brings us back to the Italian neo-realist cinema, of which both Bazin and Sadoul were admirers. Both critics had compared Becker's earlier films (in particular, *Antoine et Antoinette*) to this style: Sadoul because of the social background of the film's central couple, and Bazin because of the film's attention to the everyday details of ordinary lives.[27] Both critics discussed Becker as at least a potential *auteur* – with a world-view expressed in the realistic depiction of characters and their environments – and their discussions of *Casque d'or* develop these issues of authorship and realism in relation to the film's perceived authenticity (or lack of it).

Georges Sadoul *and* Les Lettres françaises

George Sadoul became known as a film critic after the Liberation thanks to his contributions to *Les Lettres françaises* and the publication of the first volumes of his *Histoire générale du cinéma* in 1946. He had been associated with surrealism in the 1920s and 1930s, and involved in the clandestine Communist press during the war. *Les Lettres françaises* was a left-wing publication which, along with with its sister publication, *L'Ecran français*, emerged from clandestinity in a spirit of political inclusivity, but became increasingly entrenched in a Stalinist position as the Cold War developed.[28] Critics addressed first and foremost the ideological correctness of films in their depiction of the working class, trade unionism, workers' rights and so on.

According to Laurent Marie, the relaxation of the party line after Khrushchev's 1956 denunciation of Stalin somewhat took the ground from beneath the Communist critics' unbending championing of socialist realism, leading to greater discussion of style, and even a patriotic defence of the quality tradition.[29] However, Sadoul's response to *Casque d'or* demonstrates that, already in the rigorously Stalinist early 1950s, Communist criticism was paying attention to style, and was ready to recognise brilliance of form even when the subject matter was 'doubtful'.

Sadoul's first review of *Casque d'or* appeared in *L'Ecran français* on 18 April 1952. Entitled 'Puissance de la sobriété' ('The power of sobriety'), the review highly praises the understated representation of the passionate love affair between the honest carpenter and the *gigolette* (woman of 'easy virtue') and is extremely positive compared with many French reviews. In particular, Sadoul considers what Amélie Hélie's story might have become if it had been made with Jean Gabin at the time of *Quai des brumes* or *Pépé le Moko*: 'A hero caught between Love and Death, on the point of an impossible Departure for "elsewhere", but succumbing in the end, under the weight of some metaphysical fatality, since Destiny is always stronger than men.'[30]

For Sadoul, Becker's film triumphs in the depiction of a working-class man whose difficulties are those of everyday, 'real' life – much like those encountered by the hero of *Bicycle Thieves*, for example – the portrait not of a victim of fate but of a victim of society. Becker's approach to the original material allows his film to transcend its origins in the sensational press of the 1900s, in order to attain its remarkable dignity. This is expressed in the modesty of the *mise-en-scène*, acting and dialogue that Sadoul classes as 'typically French' – and which he hopes will be applied to a more worthy subject for Becker's next film.

However, this was not to be Sadoul's final word on the film. The following week saw him revise his opinion of *Casque d'or*, decrying the bad faith the film demonstrated in its depiction of an honest craftsman as being so easily distracted from pride in his work and class solidarity.[31] Sadoul also regretted Becker's abandoning of the portrait of contemporary France that he saw as a continuation of Renoir's 1930s films. Even with these strong reservations, Sadoul was more generous to the film than many other critics (for example, Bazin, cited below), but it must be said that neither of his reviews picks up on the truly challenging aspect of the subject matter: Marie's situation and status as equal protagonist, and the depiction of the exploitation of women. For Sadoul, it seems, the class struggle pertains first and foremost to 'legitimate' (and male) workers – the exploitation of those such as prostitutes, outside of the 'official' economy (even those who worked in regulated brothels were tolerated rather than officially sanctioned), is beyond his concern. Only Sadoul's colleague Roger Boussinot does pick up on these concerns, suggesting that debates on the 'condition féminine' were being heeded at least in some revolutionary circles.

Boussinot's review is the only one to consider the feminism of the film, and to place Marie at the centre of the narrative. Though he had decried

Becker's earlier *Antoine et Antoinette* for its patronising depiction of the working classes, without considering the maturity and strength of the female protagonist,[32] this aspect now becomes the focus of his critique of *Casque d'or*, which offers a Marxist analysis of Marie's situation, and, even more astonishingly for the time, hints that her exploitation has some relevance to the contemporary situation of women in France:

> In love, in a milieu where women are bought and sold, Casque d'or lets the bidding rise but then escapes [...] Even in the worst subjection, she remains free – doubtless greatly to the honour of the real Casque d'or... yet the truth of this character is current, in this film made a few months ago.[33]

Thus, the 'social realist' critical discourse – often condemned for the narrowness of its approach – in this case has permitted Boussinot to spot an important aspect of the film that is entirely absent from either of Sadoul's reviews. For Sadoul, Marie's situation as a '*pierreuse*' (his term refers to a particularly lowly form of prostitute who solicited on building sites) is problematic because it is a cinematic cliché and not because it signifies her subjection, and her triumph is that her 'dramatic' femininity enables the spectator to forget the banality of such a role. Boussinot, on the other hand, not only condemns her sexual enslavement but also, just five years after the brothels were closed and a mere three years after the publication of *The Second Sex*, paints Marie as a contemporary woman. As we shall see, this was not an aspect of the film that was to feature greatly in the *Cahiers du cinéma* debates on the film.

André Bazin and the Cahiers du cinéma

Bazin is best known as the leader of the ciné-club and film education movements during the war, as an influential film critic and as co-founder (with Doniol-Valcroze) of *Cahiers du cinéma* – in 1951. In these various capacities he emerged as a father figure to many of the young critics who would go on to become the directors of the New Wave. Prior to 1951, Bazin's film criticism appeared in a range of publications from *Le Parisien libéré* to *La Revue du cinéma*. He was an enthusiastic cinephile who left an important theoretical contribution to debates on realism and film.[34]

If Sadoul was worried about the political 'incorrectness' of *Casque d'or*'s representation of the worker and of the period setting, André Bazin's concerns were quite different, and his initial opinion was extremely scathing. His 1952 review denounces the film as dishonest because it employs a realist aesthetic to present fictional versions of real people. For Bazin, the problem lies in the disparity between Becker's script and his *mise-en-scène*:

His story is false from A to Z...Having bored us so much with these characters...who are, in the end, conventional platitudes, Becker might have had some poor excuse if they had existed as he has presented them. He no longer has any alibi when we think that, to top it all, he has totally invented them.[35]

Thus Bazin questions the 'authenticity' of Becker's film, seeing it as a fraud, claiming through its aesthetic an authentic cachet to which it has no right, since it fails to respect the reality of the *apaches* – the 'romantic anarchy' of their world. Given Bazin's concern with the privileged relationship of cinema to the real,[36] *Casque d'or*'s fictionalising of 'real people and their actual deeds' must have seemed to him almost a betrayal of cinema itself, nothing but a con trick – an abuse of the realist aesthetic deployed to portray worthless characters and an unworthy subject.[37]

This notion, which brings together the discourses of art and the real, was to start something of a debate among *Cahiers du cinéma* critics. Jacques Doniol-Valcroze, writing in *France Observateur*, is astonished that Becker should have wasted his talent on such a worn-out subject, and again denounces the mismatch between Becker's delicate, subtle style and this melodramatic plot.[38] Jean Quéval, on the other hand, finds it to be a 'faux chef-d'œuvre' because of its lack of internal coherence – jumping too often and too suddenly from one register or tone to another, and including 'picturesque' elements which detract from the essential story of Marie and Manda's love affair.[39] These writings, which appeared in different publications but were all written by *Cahiers* critics or editors, then, show a certain conformity of opinion.

Bazin, however, dramatically revised his opinion of *Casque d'or* a few years later. Persuaded to look at the film afresh by the enthusiasm of Anderson, Truffaut and Rivette, on the occasion of a screening of the film at the Ciné-Club of Bry-sur-Marne in 1955, Bazin declared not only that he had been mistaken in his earlier assessment of the film, but that he now thought it the best and most beautiful of Becker's films:

By this, I mean that the rest of Becker's œuvre falls more or less in the realm of comedy, whereas *Casque d'or* is on the side of tragedy, with all that this genre implies of nobility and grandeur. It is – and I'm certain this time – one of the most beautiful post-war French films, and its critical semi-failure is even more unjustifiable than its commercial semi-failure.[40]

This astonishing about-turn is echoed by Quéval in 1962, declaring *Casque d'or* to be 'a success in all ways and at all levels' – Becker's best film – revising his 'inadequate' original opinion.[41] Doniol-Valcroze also changed his mind, declaring in 1960 that *Casque d'or* was 'the crown of a great film maker'.[42]

We can find further positive positions on the film printed in *Cahiers du cinéma* after 1952: Rivette and Truffaut declared to Becker that *Casque d'or* was their favourite film when they interviewed him in 1954. In his review of *Grisbi*, Truffaut argued that with each new film, Becker pushed at the boundaries of cinema: 'This movie was unfilmable four years ago; you had to have made *Casque d'or* first. It's good to make films in 1954 that were unthinkable in 1950.'[43] Lindsay Anderson stuck to his guns in a 1953 letter to the *Cahiers*, in which he claimed that the British were right about the film, and the French were wrong.[44] Truffaut reiterated his opinion in 1955, speaking of the 'stunning and continual richness of tone and the inventiveness in the detail of Becker's best film: *Casque d'or*'.[45] It would seem, then, that by the mid-1950s, the *Cahiers du cinéma* critics were in the vanguard, declaring *Casque d'or* ripe for re-evaluation. However, it was to take a further decade before the film was re-released on French screens and before it was generally declared to be a classic.

These debates support Crisp's analysis of the complexity of critical discourses at this time. *Les Lettres françaises*, often considered dogmatic in its toeing of the party line, in fact offers quite disparate views on the film, and it is the *Cahiers* critics who display the greater conformity. And even when the Stalinist line was at its most unyielding, Sadoul was able to privilege film style above subject matter, while Bazin, often seen as an aesthete first and foremost, is concerned with the subject matter's lack of 'authenticity'. For both Sadoul and Bazin, it is a question of the representation of 'truth': Sadoul finds this in Becker's refinement and perfection of style while Bazin eventually finds it in the tragedy of his characters – characters originally dismissed as 'conventional platitudes'. After Becker's death in 1960, his work did not continue to excite such polemical debate, and for many years, his films were unjustly ignored. However, the 1990s saw a resurgence in interest with new critical perspectives on Becker's films, and on *Casque d'or* in particular.

Continued life: critical views

A retrospective of Becker's work at the Locarno Festival of 1991 was followed by the re-issuing of several of his films in France in 1992, leading to a resurgence of interest in the director's work and in his best-known film, *Casque d'or*. In France, Jean Quéval's 1962 book on Becker remained the only work devoted to the director until Claude Beylie and Freddie Buache edited a selection of presentations given at the Locarno Festival. Since then, there have been several scholarly works: Valérie Vignaux and Claude Naumann have both written theses on Becker's work, and published books relating to these studies; Jean-Louis Vey has contributed a book-length study of Becker's themes and style; and, as early as 1987, Jean-Louis Tarnowski used *Casque d'or* as a major case study in his thesis on film aesthetics and theory.[46]

Further afield in Britain, *Sight and Sound* pursued Lindsay Anderson's enthusiasm for the film in a 1969 article by Gilberto Pérez Guillermo on *Le Trou* and *Casque d'or*. There are still no book-length studies in English of Becker's œuvre, though films such as *Goupi Mains Rouges* and *Touchez pas au grisbi* have attracted recent scholarly attention. As for *Casque d'or*, it has been the subject of studies as wide-ranging as Dudley Andrew's article first published in 1990 addressing the film's relation to cinematic and political history and Susan Hayward's recent analysis of the film in relation to Signoret.[47]

This section will examine some of the major points of analysis raised in these works. The continued interest in *Casque d'or* pays homage to its richness as an example of classic French cinema, but also suggests that the film continues to resonate with modern audiences. However, there are also some crucial elements that are not covered by most of these analyses, notably regarding *Casque d'or*'s contemporary context.

The majority of the French studies consider the film within an *auteurist* framework, usually within a larger project of re-evaluating Becker's œuvre, whereas the British studies tend to focus on the film itself, often exploring its intertextual resonances, for example in relation to history or the star. Within the French context, only Burch and Sellier discuss *Casque d'or*'s importance in terms of its extraordinary depiction of gender relations, but they only touch briefly on the film as part of their overview of the 1950s.[48] Paradoxically, the fact that it is the best-known of Becker's films means that it is somewhat marginalised in many discussions of his work which aim to reveal some of the more 'minor' or less well-known films. So, for example, *Casque d'or* is rarely discussed as one of Becker's 'films de couple', even though it was made in between *Edouard et Caroline* and *Rue de l'Estrapade*, and offers just as much of an exploration of heterosexual relationships as these other films, and, indeed, far more of a challenge to the misogyny of the time. Perhaps more understandably, neither does it qualify as a major study of masculine friendship – this honour is usually reserved for *Touchez pas au grisbi* and *Le Trou*.

It is largely thanks to the critics associated with the New Wave, especially François Truffaut, that *Casque d'or* came to be seen as a classic, and Becker as a post-war French *auteur*. Becker's influence on Truffaut has been commented on by many – it is certainly true that both directors share with Renoir a sympathy and warmth for their characters that lends their films an extraordinary level of humanity.[49] It is in part thanks to the preoccupation of these 'Young Turks' with aesthetic elements such as realism of *mise-en-scène* and dialogue, or minimalist performance styles, which they privileged over subject matter that Becker's films – films about 'nothing' as Bazin had described them[50] – came to be appreciated critically. And yet, as Jean-Louis Vey points out, this dominance of a purely stylistic approach means that there has been little attempt to re-examine the subject matter of Becker's films.[51] Vey sets out to redress this balance, focusing on Becker's key themes, in an attempt to elevate him beyond his reputation as the film-maker of minutiae. Though Vey's approach is still traditionally *auteurist* – looking at themes that emerge across Becker's work such as seduction, love, friendship, loyalty and betrayal, madness and death, and even on occasion relating them rather tenuously to incidents in the director's life (e.g. Micheline Presle's description of Becker as extremely seductive, his relationship with Annette Wademant, his close friendship with Renoir, and so on) – he does succeed in putting the spotlight back onto the themes of the films.

Most French discussions of Becker's work focus on his stylistic achievements. Tarnowski, for example, prefers to 'appreciate' the film as a 'work of art' rather than discuss contextual issues. He rejects theoretical approaches that draw on psychoanalysis or semiotics such as those of Christian Metz or Jean Mitry, as self-justifying and intellectually exclusive. Tarnowski, following Bazin, is for an 'aesthetic of cinema that is both theoretical and practical'.[52] However, rather disappointingly, his own discussion of *Casque d'or* does not really deliver a new approach, offering instead a textual analysis focusing on *mise-en-scène* and narrative structure. Although he perceptively examines Becker's use of contrasts to 'neutralise' melodrama, he completely ignores the film's cinematic, historical or political contexts, and his unquestioning positioning of Becker as the film's sole author forbids any discussion of the role of star persona or actors' performances in creating meaning. Thus, the fact that Marie's situation as a prostitute is sidelined in favour of her passionate love for Manda is attributed somewhat esoterically to the 'great strength of the film and Becker's work to achieve intensified contrasts',[53] rather than to Signoret's performance.

Vignaux looks for stylistic coherence across all Becker's films.[54] She describes Becker as the 'the director of duration'[55] – and focuses most closely on temporality in his works. Her analysis of *Casque d'or* therefore is most concerned with narrative construction, discussing the complexity of a plot that has been dismissed by many as thin and worn-out.[53] Vignaux, like Tarnowski, points to the tight cause and effect chain of the film. The fact that we join each scene after it has begun increases the pace, linking Manda's 'fate' to the march of time, rather than to some preordained tragic destiny.[57] Here again, the analysis of *Casque d'or* is part of a wider investigation of Becker's 'implicit aesthetic'. Although Vignaux places more emphasis than other French critics on the historical and cultural contexts in which Becker's films were made, she, like many other commentators, fails to make the connection between *Casque d'or* and France's recent history, notably the Occupation and questions of collaboration and resistance.

This lack of critical discussion of the relevance of Becker's films to the time and place in which they are set, beyond their 'documentary' interest as representations of specific *milieux*, suggests that many critics are happy to accept the contemporary judgement on the film as a costume drama that did not fit its age – an 'exercice de style'. Even Andrew's perceptive analysis of the film as an elegy to lost left-wing values states that '[o]ne looks in vain for an allegory of the Fourth Republic or of the Cold War. The broadcast of the film, like most films of the day, reaches no further than the sphere of the cinematic.'[58] Only Hayward, picking up on Andrew's analysis, relates *Casque d'or*'s evocation of working-class values of solidarity, friendship and loyalty to the decline of the Left in post-war France, the sidelining of the PCF due to both American and Soviet intervention in French politics, and the return of the Right, leading to the amnesty in 1952, which allowed former Vichyites to hold positions of power once again.[59] Of course, it is true that *Casque d'or* does not offer an analogy of the immediate problems facing the Fourth Republic – most obviously France's relationship with her colonies and Indochina in particular at this time. However, there are elements in the film that are clearly comments on 1940s France – most especially the character of Leca, who can be seen as embodying the collaboration, denunciation and profiteering that were rife during the Occupation. Vey highlights the theme of betrayal in Becker's work, but rather extraordinarily attributes it entirely to the personal betrayal that Becker experienced by his friends André Halley des Fontaines and Jean Renoir over *Le Crime de Monsieur Lange* in 1935, failing even to mention the Occupation. Vey argues that Leca's treachery is ultimately triumphant, since Manda goes to the scaffold believing that Marie has betrayed him with Leca, unaware that she is watching from above. However, there is a more positive reading of the film's ending made possible by Marie's activity. Even though Manda has no chance to speak to Marie, he has seen her and she has helped him to escape, thus proving her loyalty. He therefore knows, when he finds her slippers at Leca's house, that they represent not a betrayal on Marie's part, but a further outrage of Leca's. Manda's murder of Leca, then, becomes an act of liberation, a final gift to Marie of her freedom, as well as an act of revenge for Raymond's death.

Becker's use of such details as the slippers (they recur as an indicator of intimacy in *Montparnasse 19*) is discussed by Gilberto Pérez Guillermo in a 1969 article on *Casque d'or* and *Le Trou*.[60] For Pérez Guillermo, Becker's 'selection and heightening of physical detail' – for example, the cheese Marie eats straight from Leca's knife and the bowl of coffee Manda takes to Marie the morning after they have made love, but also the sound of the straps that bind Manda and the gleaming blade of the guillotine in the execution sequence – lend the film a materiality. The fact that these 'moments which had seemed solid and indestructible' prove in the end to be as ephemeral as the final shot of the lovers disappearing into the distance is what, according to Pérez Guillermo, 'gives the close of the film much of its peculiar poignancy of loss'.[61]

This analysis of the final shot of the film as 'an image of loss' brings us back to the Bazinian concept of cinema itself as 'a machine for regaining lost time the better to lose it once again'.[62] Bazin wrote this phrase about Nicole Védrès' film *Paris 1900* – a documentary on the Belle Epoque made from footage from the period. Bazin argues that Védrès' film evokes memories that do not belong to the spectator, 'realising the paradox of an objective past, a memory that is outside our consciousness'. We could argue that *Casque d'or* does likewise, firstly through the authenticity of the characters and the historical reconstruction and, then, in the final shot of the film – this image of loss – which inscribes the whole within the realm of memory.

For Dudley Andrew, the collective memory that *Casque d'or* taps into is that of the Left – a nostalgia for a bygone age of 'professionalism, forthrightness and sincerity' that has increased in the years since the film's release, given the further remove of our own age from these values.[63] Andrew compares *Casque d'or* to the 1930s films of Carné–Prévert and of Renoir and his team, as well as to the quality cinema of the 1950s, in order to examine why Becker's film seems so cut off from its own time. He does not, however, look critically at critics' refusal to look at the film in relation to its present, or even, from a perspective endowed with hindsight, of the future. Signoret, after all, claimed in 1973 that it was because *Casque d'or* was *ahead* of its time that it was not fully appreciated in the early 1950s. It is essential to remember that the period of the Fourth Republic was marked by heavy censorship in France, a fact commented on by Becker, Truffaut and Rivette:

> Rivette and Truffaut: It would be impossible in France to address subjects such as the corruption of politicians, civil servants, etc… Becker: That's right. […] We don't even have the right to show a postman accepting money to send a letter astray.[64]

Seen in this light, the past setting of *Casque d'or* that permits Becker to show the institutional corruption of Leca and 'his cop', Inspector Juliani, as a way of life becomes more than a nostalgic rebuke to a degenerate present. It becomes a means of representing the present (and the recent past) in at least as incisive and critical a way as Becker's depictions of contemporary Paris life. And the fact that 'Casque d'or struck critics in 1952 as a film cut off from social life and even, on account of its deliberate rhythm, cut off from the sensibility of what was becoming the jazz age'[65] could be said to reveal an unwillingness to see on the part of the critics, rather than the short-sightedness of the film.

Notes

1   Signoret: *La Nostalgie...* , p. 118.
2   Simsi, Simon, *Ciné-Passion 7: Sème art et industrie de 1945 à 2000* (Paris: Dixit, 2000). All box office figures are taken from this volume unless otherwise stated.
3   Frank, Nino, '*Casque d'or* par Jacques Becker', *Arts*, 1 May 1952. See also Quéval: '*Casque d'or*': Doniol-Valcroze: 'Les Cheveux sur la soupe'; Magnan: 'Le Cinéma: *Casque d'or* de Jacques Becker'.
4   Frank: '*Casque d'or* par Jacques Becker'.
5   Frank: '*Casque d'or* par Jacques Becker'.
6   See Magnan: 'Le Cinéma: *Casque d'or*', and Lauwick: '*Casque d'or*'.
7   Magnan: 'Le Cinéma: *Casque d'or*'.
8   For example, Magnan, 'Le Cinéma: *Casque d'or*'; Quéval: '*Casque d'or*'; Quéval, Jean, 'Pavane pour apaches défunts', *Cahiers du cinéma* 3.13 (June 1952), pp. 71–72, p. 72.
9   See Quéval: '*Casque d'or*'; Magnan: 'Le Cinéma: *Casque d'or*'.
10 Lang, André, 'Les Nouveaux Films: *Casque d'or*', *France-Soir*, 19 April 1952.
11 See Magnan: 'Le Cinéma, *Casque d'or*', Doniol-Valcroze: 'Les Cheveux sur la soupe', and Quéval: 'Pavane pour apaches défunts'. See also Bazin, André, '*Casque d'or*', *Le Parisien libéré*, 24 April 1952, cited in Naumann: *Jacques Becker*, pp. 164–165; Charensol, Georges, '*Casque d'or*', cited in Naumann: *Jacques Becker*, p. 167.
12 Anon., 'No title', *Manchester Guardian*, 6 September 1952; Anon., 'No title', *Spectator*, 5 September 1952; Anon., '*Casque d'or*', *The Times*, 8 September 1952; Anon., 'French realism', *Times Educational Supplement*, 26 September 1952; Lambert, Gavin, '*Golden Marie*', *Evening Standard*, 4 September 1952; Lambert, Gavin, 'The movies: *Casque d'or* at the Academy', *New Statesman*, 13 September 1952; Lejeune, C. A., 'No title', *Observer*, 7 September 1952; Mosley, Leonard, 'No Title', *Daily Express*, 29 August 1952; Powell, Dilys, '*Golden Marie*', *Sunday Times*, 7 September 1952; R., D., 'No title', *Sunday Picture*, 7 September 1952; Whitley, Reg, 'No title', *Daily Mirror*, 5 September 1952; Winnington, Richard, 'No title', *News Chronicle*, 6 September 1952.
13 Anon., '*Casque d'or*', *Sunday Dispatch*, 7 September 1952; Anon., 'No title', *Daily Worker*, 6 September 1952; Bowman, George, 'No title', *Evening News*, 5 September 1952; Grant, Elspeth, 'It's all just a wee bit squalid', *Daily Graphic*, 5 September 1952; Nash, Ray, 'No title', *Star*, no date.

14   Magdalaney, Fred, 'Golden Marie', *Daily Mail*, 5 September 1952; Mannock, P. L., 'No Title', *Daily Herald*, 5 September 1952; Gibbs, P., 'Versatility', *Daily Telegraph*, 8 September 1952.

15   Magdalaney: 'No title', *Daily Mail*; Bowman: 'No title', *Evening News*; Grant: 'It's all just a wee bit squalid'; Anon., 'No title', *Spectator*; Mannock: 'No title', *Daily Herald*; D. R.: 'No title', *Sunday Picture*; Lejeune: 'No title', *Observer*; and Gibbs: 'Versatility'. All except Bowman prefer *Casque d'or* of the two films.

16   See Winnington: 'No Title', *News Chronicle* and Grant: 'It's all just a wee bit squalid'.

17   Lambert: 'Golden Marie'.

18   Powell: 'Golden Marie'.

19   Powell: 'Golden Marie'.

20   Anderson, Lindsay, 'The Current Cinema: *Casque d'or* (*Golden Marie*)', *Sight and Sound* 22.2 (October–December 1952), pp. 75–77, p. 75.

21   Bazin, André, 'Autocritique', *Les Cahiers du cinéma* 50 (August–September 1955), p. 35.

22   Anderson, Lindsay, 'Lettre anglaise sur Becker', *Les Cahiers du cinéma* 28 (November 1953), pp. 31–35.

23   Vignaux: *Jacques Becker*, pp. 134–135.

24   Crisp: *The Classic French Cinema*, pp. 233–265.

25   Crisp: *The Classic French Cinema*, pp. 235–238.

26   See Crisp: *The Classic French Cinema*, pp. 240–250 for a discussion of the extent of the debates surrounding the concept of realism in cinema.

27   Bazin: '*Antoine et Antoinette*' and Sadoul, Georges, '*Antoine et Antoinette*', *Les Lettres françaises*, 3 November 1947, cited in Naumann: *Jacques Becker*, pp. 158–159. See also Sadoul: 'Puissance de la sobriété'.

28   Baecque, Antoine de, *La Cinéphilie: Invention d'un regard, histoire d'une culture 1944–1968* (Paris: Fayard, 2003), pp. 63–66.

29   Marie, Laurent, 'Le Chêne et le roseau: The French Communist critics and the New Wave', in Elizabeth Ezra and Sue Harris (eds), *France in Focus: Film and National Identity* (Oxford and New York: Berg, 2000), pp. 43–60, esp. p. 44.

30   Sadoul: 'Puissance de la sobriété'.

31   Signoret: *La Nostalgie…*, p. 117.

32   Boussinot, Roger, '*Antoine et Antoinette*', *Action*, 5 November 1947.

33   Boussinot, Roger, 'Simone Signoret dans *Casque d'or*', *L'Ecran français*, 23 April 1952, p. 10.

34   See Baecque: *La Cinéphilie*, pp. 33–61.

35   Bazin: '*Casque d'or*'.

36   Bazin, André, 'The ontology of the photographic image', in André Bazin *What is Cinema?*, vol. 1, ed. and trans. by Hugh Gray (Berkeley, Los Angeles and London: University of California Press, 1967), pp. 9–16.

37   Bazin: '*Casque d'or*'.

38   Doniol-Valcroze: 'Les Cheveux sur la soupe'.

39   Quéval: 'Pavane pour apaches défunts', p. 72.

40   Bazin: 'Autocritique'.

41   Quéval, Jean, *Jacques Becker* (Paris: Editions Seghers, 1962), pp. 37 and 51.

42   Doniol-Valcroze, writing in *France Observateur*, 25 February 1960; cited in *L'Avant-scène cinéma* 43, December 1964, p. 61.

43   Truffaut: 'The rogues are weary', p. 29.

44   Anderson: 'Lettre anglaise sur Becker', p. 31.

45   Truffaut, François, '*Ali Baba* et la "politique des auteurs"', *Cahiers du cinéma* 44 (February 1955), pp. 45–47.

46   Quéval: *Jacques Becker*; Beylie, Claude and Freddy Buache (eds), *Jacques Becker* (Locarno: Editions du Festival de Locarno, 1991); Vey, Jean-Louis, *Jacques Becker ou la fausse évidence* (Lyon: Aléas, 1995); Vignaux: *Jacques Becker*; Naumann: *Jacques Becker*; Tarnowski: *Essais d'esthétique et de philosophie*.

47   Andrew: '*Casque d'or, casquettes*'; Pérez Guillermo, Gilberto, 'Jacques Becker: two films', *Sight and Sound* 38.3 (Summer 1969), pp. 142–147; Hayward: *Simone Signoret*, esp. pp. 96–99 and 110–120; Hewitt, Nicholas, 'Gabin, *Grisbi* and 1950s France', *Studies in French Cinema* 4.1 (2004), pp. 65–75; Sim, Gregory, 'Returning to the fold: questions of ideology in Jacques Becker's *Goupi Mains Rouges* (1942)', *French Cultural Studies* 8 (2002), pp. 5–31.

48   Burch and Sellier: *La Drôle de guerre des sexes*, pp. 262–264.

49   See Andrew: '*Casque d'or, casquettes*', p. 113 and Giavarini, Laurence and Camille Taboulay, 'Becker, le couturier', *Cahiers du cinéma* 454 (April 1992), pp. 60–71, p. 60.

50   Bazin: '*La Rue de l'Estrapade*'.

51   Vey: *Jacques Becker*, p. 15.

52   Tarnowski: *Essais d'esthétique et de philosophie*, pp. 135–138.

53   Tarnowski: *Essais d'esthétique et de philosophie*, p. 162.

54   Vignaux: *Jacques Becker*, p. 9.

55   Vignaux: *Jacques Becker*, p. 236.

56   But not by Truffaut, who recognised the brilliance of the ending in the way it sustains dramatic intensity. See Truffaut: 'De vraies moustaches'.

57   Vignaux: *Jacques Becker*, pp. 128–130.

58   Andrew: '*Casque d'or, casquettes*', p. 118.

59   Hayward: *Simone Signoret*, pp. 98–99. Hayward cites the example of Antoine Pinay, a former member of Pétain's Vichy government, who was appointed prime minister in 1952.

60   Pérez Guillermo: 'Jacques Becker: two films', pp. 143–144.

61   Pérez Guillermo: 'Jacques Becker: two films', p. 144.

62   Bazin, 'Nicole Védrès: Paris 1900'; cited in Smith, Douglas, '"A world that accords with our desires"?: realism, desire and death in André Bazin's film criticism', *Studies in French Cinema* 4.2 (2004), pp. 93–102, p. 102.

63   Andrew: '*Casque d'or, casquettes*', p. 113.

64   Rivette and Truffaut: 'Entretien avec Jacques Becker', p. 16.

65   Andrew: '*Casque d'or, casquettes*', p. 117.

Conclusion

In its evocation of several lost pasts, *Casque d'or* draws its power from the nostalgic solace it offers the spectator: on a narrative level, with Marie and Manda's poignant love affair; on a stylistic level, with the evocative depiction of the Belle Epoque; and on a cinematic level, with the suggestion of a warm, collective type of film-making, which disappeared with the increased regulation of the French film industry in the post-war years. *Casque d'or*, then, offers a sort of 'collective memory' to a nation busy forgetting its recent past. The fact that there is such a myth surrounding the making of the film – in an atmosphere of 'joy and love' – suggests that this collectivity was unusual at the time.

However, *Casque d'or* is not entirely lost in the mists of nostalgia. We have seen how far ahead of its time *Casque d'or* was in its representation of gender and of heterosexual relationships, but there is more. Becker's characters are truly post-war characters. They make their own decisions and thus determine their own future. Their adversaries are human and there is no suggestion of fatalistic doom surrounding them: compare the agency of *Casque d'or*'s characters with the earlier *Les Portes de la nuit*, where the characters are helpless in the face of destiny, heavy-handedly personified by the harmonica-playing tramp (Jean Vilar). Both films may end in tragedy (in *Les Portes de la nuit*, it is the female character who dies, shot by 'accident' by her jealous ex-lover) but in *Casque d'or* this is not the result of chance, but of conscious decisions. And, as a costume drama, Becker's film is innovative in the way that the paintings of the Impressionists had been, moving the action out of the salons and boudoirs of the wealthy to focus on lower-class and marginal districts of the 'people'. And contrary to that other popular costume drama, *Les Enfants du paradis*, the people are shown in a non-theatrical *milieu* – as ordinary and rooted in the real. Furthermore, unlike many Belle Epoque films of the late 1940s and early 1950s, *Casque d'or* is a costume drama that demands that we look beyond the costumes, at the characters. And, finally, in its insistence on the collective work of film-making, Becker's film also looks forward to the New Wave. The New Wave is often seen as the age when the *auteur* – understood as the individual 'artist'

– triumphed. But it was also a time of a return to the teamwork of film-making through formal and informal collaborations: for example, Chabrol, Truffaut and Godard provided one another with scripts (which were then considerably re-written); partnerships such as those between Godard and cinematographer Raoul Coutard, Truffaut and Jean-Pierre Léaud, or Louis Malle and Jeanne Moreau, were of crucial importance; not forgetting the collectivity of the *Cahiers du cinéma*, which nurtured so many of these directors.

Casque d'or, then, is a pivotal film, right in the middle of Becker's career, as well as of the century. Despite its period setting, it offers a remarkable synthesis of the French realist film tradition, which runs from Feuillade through the 1930s to the New Wave and beyond – a tradition that is still very much alive today. It also contains the most luminous and enduring image of Simone Signoret as Marie, sensual yet tough, a pre-feminist icon for the 1950s. Like its director and its star, *Casque d'or* is deeply rooted in French cinema.

Appendix 1: Credits

Crew

Director: Jacques Becker

Production: Speva Films and Paris-Film-Production
Executive producer: Michel Safra
Producer: Henri Baum
Assistant producer: Ulrich Picard
Production administrator: Robert Demollière
Production secretary: Simone Lambert

Scriptwriters: Jacques Becker and Jacques Companeez
Dialogue: Jacques Becker

Director of photography: Robert Lefebvre
Camera operator: Jean-Marie Maillols
Assistant camera operators: Gilbert Sarthre and Gaston Muller
Crane operator: Francis Rivolan
First assistant director: Marcel Camus
Second assistant director: Michel Clément
Script girl: Colette Crochot
Editor: Marguerite Houllé-Renoir
Assistant editor: Geneviève Vaury

Production designer: Jean d'Eaubonne; assistants: Marc Frédéric and Alfred Marpaux
Set manager: Maurice Barnathan
Painter: Alfred Marpaux
Set dresser: Emile Dechelle

Costume designer: Mayo
Costumes: Marcelle Desvignes

Corsets: Marie-Rose Lebigot
Wardrobe: Georgette Fillon
Make-up: Boris Karabanoff and M. Vernadet
Hair stylist: Alex Archambault
Accessories: Maurice Terrasse

Original music: Georges Van Parys
Music: Jean-Baptiste Clément ('Le Temps des cerises')

Sound engineer: Antoine Petitjean; assistants: Aubiroux and Gaston Ancessi

Location manager: Charles Chieusse
Unit manager: Louis Théron; assistant: Léo Frémery
Chief electrician: André Tixier

Still photographer: Henry Thibault
Press officer: Jean Mounier
Publisher: Maurice Vendair

Distribution: Discina (with *Éclair* journal)
Colour: Black and white
Production format: 35mm
Sound format: Optiphone (mono)
Running time: 96 mins
Filmed at: Paris-Studio-Cinéma
Exteriors: Annet-sur-Marne, Belleville
Production began: 24 September 1951
Release date (Paris): 16 April 1952

Cast:

Simone Signoret	Marie Casque d'or
Serge Reggiani	Georges Manda
Claude Dauphin	Félix Leca
Raymond Bussières	Raymond
William Sabatier	Roland
Gaston Modot	Danard
Loleh Bellon	Léonie Danard
Paul Azaïs	Ponsard

Jean Clarieux	Paul
Emile Genevois	Billy
Claude Castaing	Frédo
Pierre Goutas	Guillaume
Dominique Davray	Julie
Roland Lesaffre	Anatole the waiter
Pâquerette	Anatole's grandmother
Daniel Mendaille	Owner of the *guinguette*
Fernand Trignol	The 'patron' of the Ange Gabriel
Yvonne Yma	The 'patronne' of the Ange Gabriel
Odette Barencey	Mère Eugène
Yette Lucas	Mère Adèle
Paul Barge	Inspector Juliani
Tony Corteggiani	The commissaire
Marcel Melrac	Gendarme
Marcel Rouze	Gendarme
Léon Pauléon	The driver
Roger Vincent	The doctor
Pomme	The concierge
Suzanne Grey	A whore
Odette Talazac	Middle-class woman at the *guinguette*
André Méliès	Middle-class man at the *guinguette*
Raphaël Patorni	Chic client at the Ange Gabriel 1
Léon Bary	Chic client at the Ange Gabriel 2
Jean Degrave	Chic client at the Ange Gabriel 3

Solange Certin; Jacqueline Danno; Anne Beressy; Marianne Bergue; Jacqueline Canterelle; Gisèle Delzen; Simone Jarnac; Jacqueline Marbaut; Christiane Minazzoli; Martine Arden; Joëlle Bernard; Marianne Borgue; Solange Cortain; Abel Coulon; Max Lancourt; Pierre Leproux; Julien Maffre; Bobby Mercier; Louis Moret; René Pascal; Raymond Raynal; Henri Couttet; Jean Berton; Roger Dalphin

Appendix 2: Sequence breakdown

Temporality	Sequences	Place	Duration	No of shots	ASL
	Opening Credits		1m 37s		
Section 1			44m 22s	348	7.6s
Day 1	Sequence 1: Part 1 – The river then the *guinguette*. Marie and her friends. Marie dances with Roland. Part 2 – Raymond introduces Manda to friends. Marie and Manda dance. Manda and Roland fight.	River/ *Guin- guette*	10m 48s	87 (1–87)	7.4s
Day 2 – Morning	Sequence 2: Streets of Belleville – gang members looking for Marie. Find her at Julie's place.	Belle- ville	3m 16s	22 (88– 109)	8.9s
	Sequence 3: Part 1 – Chez Leca. Marie and Leca discuss Roland. Leca offers to buy her. Part 2 – The division of the spoils. Frédo has kept some back. Leca disciplines him.	Chez Leca	8m 58s (4m 45s) (4m 13s)	61 38 (110– 170)	8.8s
Lunchtime	Sequence 4: Marie in cab. Manda, Danard and Léonie at lunch. Cab driver calls	Belle- ville/ atelier Danard	2m 51s	36 (171– 206)	4.8s

Temporality	Sequences	Place	Duration	No of shots	ASL
	Manda. The couple are reunited on the wasteland outside the workshop: they kiss. Léonie interrupts, furious. Marie learns Manda is engaged. Léonie calls Marie a *putain*. Marie slaps Manda.				
Day 2 – Evening	Sequence 5: Upper-class 'tourists' arrive. The *apaches* are present, and Leca with 'his cop'. Roland dances with a rich woman. Marie and Julie make an entrance. Manda arrives to take Marie away.	L'Ange Gabriel	7m 33s	41 (207–247)	11s
	Sequence 6: Fight in the courtyard. Leca acts as 'referee'. Manda kills Roland. Police arrive (informed by the waiter, Anatole) and discover Roland's body.	Court-yard and Ange Gabriel	10m 56s	101 (248–348)	6.5s
Section 2			22m 52s	125	11s
Day 3	Sequence 7: Manda's departure. Danard offers him money,	Atelier Danard	2m 40s	13 (349–361)	12.3s

Temporality	Sequences	Place	Duration	No of shots	ASL
	Manda refuses. Child brings him a note from 'Raymond'.	Belle- ville			
Day 4	Sequence 8: Part 1 – Joinville, Mère Eugène's farm. The river, Marie rows up to the sleeping Manda and awakens him.				
	Part 2 – Awakening – Manda gets up first. Then Marie wakes up. Reassured by his stuff on the chair. Coffee with Mère Eugène. Part 3 – Marie and Manda walk in forest – birds singing. Marie sits down and invites him to kiss her.	Join- ville	7m 56s	49 (362– 410)	9.7
Meanwhile…	Sequence 9: Leca in Belleville. L'Ange Gabriel. We learn of Anatole's death – collection for his grandmother. Frédo tells Leca where Marie and Manda are, Raymond overhears. Leca denounces Raymond to Insp. Juliani.	L'Ange Gabriel	4m 40s	27 (411– 437)	10.4
Day 5	Sequence 10: Part 1 – Marie and Manda witness the wedding.	Join- ville	7m 36s	36 (438– 473)	12.7

Temporality	Sequences	Place	Duration	No of shots	ASL
	Part 2 – Leca tells Manda that Raymond was arrested yesterday. Part 3 – Mère Eugène's – Manda thinking about Raymond. Marie and Manda go				
Day 6 – Early morning	to bed. Part 4 – Marie wakes up – Manda's stuff not there any more. Has left the paper for her with details of Raymond's arrest.				
Section 3			23m 56s + 29s	202	7.1s
	Sequence 11: Part 1 – Newspaper – Leca and gang discussing Raymond's arrest. Part 2 – Marie arrives at Leca's place. Asks him to help. Leca rapes her.	Chez Leca	3m 36s	24 (474– 497)	9s
	Sequence 12: Police station. Manda gives himself up. Raymond finds out it was Leca who denounced him.	Police stn	3m 16s	25 (498– 522)	7.8s
Afternoon (later same day or next day? Temporality here not so clearly indicated	Sequence 13: Marie brings Leca paper – news of Manda's transfer. Leca betrays her and then beats her.	Chez Leca	1m 20s	7 (523– 529)	11.4s

Temporality	Sequences	Place	Duration	No of shots	ASL
– is Marie's newspaper an evening edition, or the following morning's?)	Sequence 14: The prisoners are being transported to La Santé. Marie brings cakes and cigarettes.	Belle-ville	2m 09s	13 (530–542)	9.9s
	Sequence 15: In the 'black maria' – Raymond tells Manda that Leca betrayed them.	Prison vehicle	1m 32s	12 (543–554)	7.7s
	Sequence 16: Marie waits outside the prison, bd Arago. Helps Manda and Raymond escape – Raymond shot.	La Santé	1m 53s	21 (555–575)	5.4
	Sequence 17: L'Ange Gabriel. Manda brings Raymond there.	L'Ange Gabriel	1m 27s	14 (576–589)	6.2s
	Sequence 18: Manda goes to Leca's house. Leca not there.	Chez Leca	1m 34s	12 (590–601)	7.7s
	Sequence 19: L'Ange Gabriel. Doctor for Raymond. Raymond dies. Leca arrives, then leaves.	L'Ange Gabriel	0m 58s	15 (602–616)	7.8s
	Sequence 20: Manda searching for Leca. Follows him to the police station. Shoots him down in the courtyard.	Belle-ville Police stn	2m 07s	31 (617–647)	4.1s
Day 7 – Before dawn occurs some time after day 6.	Sequence 21: Boulevard Arago, hotel and then prison courtyard. Marie and Paul in *fiacre*,	Bd Arago/ Hotel/ La Santé	4m 04s	28 (648–675)	8.7s

Temporality	Sequences	Place	Duration	No of shots	ASL
Ellipsis signalled by dissolve to black, but non-diegetic music is continuous End section III	arrive at hotel. Climb to room w. view. Execution of Manda – Marie watching.	courtyard			
Epilogue: outside the temporal logic of the film	*Guinguette*, day. Marie and Manda dancing to 'Le Temps des cerises'.	*Guinguette*	0m 29	1 (676)	29s
	End credits.				

*ASLs rounded up to 1 decimal place.

Total length (excluding opening and closing credits): 1h 31m 39s
Total number of shots: 676
Average shot length (ASL): 8.1 seconds

Main spaces:
Belleville: Leca's house, L'Ange Gabriel, Danard's workshop;
the countryside: the *guinguette*, Joinville and Mère Eugène's farm;
spaces of the law: the police station, or the 'black maria', boulevard Arago and La Santé prison; spaces of transit: the streets, in *fiacres*.

Appendix 3: Filmographies and awards

Jacques Becker: filmography as director

1935   *Le Commissaire est bon enfant* (with Pierre Prévert) [short]

1935   *Une tête qui rapporte* (aka *Tête de Turc*) [short]

1938   *La Grande espérance* [documentary]

1940   *L'Or du Cristobal/Cristobal's Gold* (abandoned; film finished by Jean Stelli)

1942   *Dernier atout*

1943   *Goupi Mains Rouges/It happened at the Inn*

1945   *Falbalas/Paris Frills*

1947   *Antoine et Antoinette/Antoine and Antoinette*

1949   *Rendez-vous de juillet/Rendezvous in July*

1951   *Edouard et Caroline/Edouard and Caroline*

1952   *Casque d'or/Golden Marie/Golden Helmet*

1953   *Rue de l'Estrapade/Françoise steps out*

1954   *Touchez pas au grisbi/Hands off the loot*

1954   *Ali Baba et les quarante voleurs/Ali Baba and the forty thieves*

1957   *Les Aventures d'Arsène Lupin/The Adventures of Arsène Lupin*

1958   *Montparnasse 19/The Lovers of Montparnasse*

1960   *Le Trou/The Hole/The Night Watch* (USA)

Prior to directing his own films, Becker had a considerable career as an assistant director. His work made a substantial technical and artistic contribution to the following films of Jean Renoir:

1932   *La Nuit du carrefour*

1932   *Boudu sauvé des eaux*

1933   *Chotard et compagnie*

1934   *Madame Bovary*

1936   *La Vie est à nous* (released 1946)

1936   *Une partie de campagne*

1936   *Les Bas-fonds*

1937   *La Grande illusion*
1938   *La Marseillaise*

He also worked on one film for Albert Valentin:

1940   *L'Héritier des Mondésir*

Becker also made a few brief but notable appearances in front of the camera:

Le Bled (Renoir, 1929) as an agricultural worker
Boudu sauvé des eaux (Renoir, 1932) as a poet
Chotard et compagnie (Renoir, 1933) as a guest at a ball
Le Commissaire est bon enfant (Becker and Prévert, 1935) as an officer cadet.
La Vie est à nous (Renoir, 1936) as an unemployed man
Les Bas-fonds (Renoir, 1936) as a man out walking
La Grande illusion (Renoir, 1937) as an English officer

Awards for *Casque d'or*

1953   BAFTA for Best Foreign Actress, UK, for Simone Signoret
1956   Silver Ribbon – Best Director of a Foreign Film, awarded by the Italian National Syndicate of Film Journalists

1953   Nominated for BAFTA for Best Film from any source
1979   Voted third-best film, French Academy of Cinematographic Arts and Techniques

Other awards for Jacques Becker

1947   Best Film, Cannes, for *Antoine et Antoinette*
1949   Louis Delluc prize for *Rendez-vous de juillet*
1951   Critics' Award for *Rendez-vous de juillet*, French Syndicate of Cinema Critics
1961   Critics' Award for *Le Trou*, French Syndicate of Cinema Critics
1962   Jussi Awards, Diploma of Merit for *Le Trou*

1956   Nominated for Golden Bear, Berlin International Film Festival, for *Les Aventures d'Arsène Lupin*

Appendix 4: Bibliography

Anderson, Katherine, 'A Sign of her times: the young Simone Signoret as star', unpublished MA essay, University of Warwick, 1998

Anderson, Lindsay, 'The current cinema: *Casque d'or* (*Golden Marie*)', *Sight and Sound* 22.2 (October–December 1952), pp. 75–77

Anderson, Lindsay, 'Lettre anglaise sur Becker', *Les Cahiers du cinéma* 28 (November 1953), pp. 31–35

Andrew, Dudley, '*Casque d'or, casquettes*, a cask of aging wine: Jacques Becker's *Casque d'or* (1952)' in Susan Hayward and Ginette Vincendeau (eds), *French Film: Texts and Contexts* 2nd edn (London and New York: Routledge, 2000), pp. 112–126

Andrew, Dudley, *Mists of Regret: Culture and sensibility in classic French film* (Princeton, NJ: Princeton University Press, 1995)

Anon., '*Casque d'or*', *Sunday Dispatch*, 7 September 1952

Anon., '*Casque d'or*', *The Times*, 8 September 1952

Anon., '*Elle* enquête dans les grandes villes de France: Nous voulons nous marier disent les jeunes', *Elle*, no. 324, 11 February 1952

Anon., 'Etes-vous celle que l'on épouse?', *Elle*, no 317, 24 December 1951

Anon., 'French realism', *Times Educational Supplement*, 26 September 1952

Anon., 'No title', *Daily Worker*, 6 September 1952

Anon., 'No title', *Manchester Guardian*, 6 September 1952

Anon., 'No title', *Spectator*, 5 September 1952

Anon., 'Serge Reggiani', *Unifrance Film*, no date (BFI microjacket)

Anon., 'Serge Reggiani', *The Times*, 28 July 2004, p. 53

Baecque, Antoine de, *La Cinéphilie: Invention d'un regard, histoire d'une culture 1944–1968* (Paris: Fayard, 2003)

Baecque, Antoine de and Serge Toubiana, *François Truffaut* (Paris: Gallimard, 1997)

Bakhtin, Mikhail, 'Forms of time and of the chronotope in the novel' in *The Dialogic Imagination: Four Essays*, trans. Caryl Emerson and Michael Holquist (Austin: University of Texas Press, 1981), pp. 84–258

La Bande à Bonnot, http://www.chez.com/durru/bonnot/bande.htm. Accessed 7 June 2005]

Bazin, André, 'Autocritique', *Les Cahiers du cinéma* 50 (August–September 1955), p. 35

Bazin, André, *What is Cinema?* (2 vols.), ed. and trans. by Hugh Gray (Berkeley, Los Angeles and London: University of California Press, 1967–1971)

Bazin, André, *Le Cinéma de la Libération à la Nouvelle Vague*, ed. J. Narboni (Paris: Cahiers du cinéma, 1998)

Beaume, Georges, 'Serge Reggiani, sera un jour le successeur de Pierre Fresnay', *Cinémonde*, 17 October 1952, pp. 7–9

Beauvoir, Simone de, *Le Deuxième sexe*, 2 vols. (Paris: Gallimard, 1949)

Becker, Jacques, '*Casque d'or*', *L'Avant-scène cinéma* 43 (December 1964), pp. 7–60

Bellanger, Claude, Jacques Godechot, Pierre Guiral and Fernand Terrou (eds), *Histoire générale de la presse française: vol. 3 1871–1940* (5 vols) (Paris: Presses Universitaires de France, 1972)

Bergstrom, Janet, 'Renouer: *French Cancan*, ou le retour de Jean Renoir en France', trans. by Christian-Marc Bosséno, *Vertigo* 21 (July 2001), pp. 157–166

Bergut, Bob, 'Comment faire la conquête morale de Serge Reggiani', *L'Ecran français* no. 271, 18 September 1950, pp. 4–5

Beylie, Claude and Freddy Buache (eds), *Jacques Becker* (Locarno: Editions du Festival de Locarno, 1991)

Billard, Pierre, *L'Age classique du cinéma français: du cinéma parlant à la nouvelle vague* (Paris: Flammarion, 1995)

Bondanella, Peter, *Italian Cinema: From Neorealism to the Present* (New York: Frederick Ungar, 1983)

Boussinot, Roger, '*Antoine et Antoinette*', *Action*, 5 November 1947

Boussinot, Roger, 'Simone Signoret dans *Casque d'or*' *L'Ecran français*, 23 April 1952, p.10

Bowman, George, 'No Title', *Evening News*, 5 September 1952

Brossat, Alain, *Les Tondues: Un carnaval moche* (Paris: Manya, 1992)

Bruzzi, Stella, *Undressing Cinema: Clothing and identity in the movies* (London and New York: Routledge, 1997)

Burch, Noel and Geneviève Sellier, *La Drôle de guerre des sexes du cinéma français 1930–1956* (Paris: Nathan, 1996)

Buss, Robin, *French Film Noir* (London: Marion Boyars, 2001)

Butler, Judith, *Gender Trouble: Feminism and the Subversion of Identity* (London and New York: Routledge, 1990)

Butler, Judith, *Bodies that Matter: On the Discursive Limits of 'Sex'* (London and New York, Routledge, 1993)

Carrey, Claude 'Serge Reggiani: Coup de foudre pour "le maudit"', *Télérama*, 25 February 1968, pp. 20–21

Chapuy, Armand, *Martine Carol filmée par Christian-Jaque : un phénomène du cinéma populaire* (Paris: Harmattan, 2001)

Chevalier, Louis, *Montmartre du plaisir et du crime* (Paris: Robert Laffont, 1980)

Chevrie, Marc, 'Un pur cinéaste', *Cahiers du cinéma* no. 378 (December 1985), pp. 48–53

Corbin, Alain, *Women for Hire: Prostitution and sexuality in France after 1850*, trans. by Alan Sheridan (Cambridge, MA and London: Harvard University Press, 1990)

Crisp, Colin, *The Classic French Cinema 1930–1960* (London: I.B. Tauris, 1993)

David, Catherine, *Simone Signoret ou la mémoire partagée* (Paris: Robert Laffont, 1990)

Doane, Mary Ann, *Femmes Fatales: Feminism, film theory and psychoanalysis* (New York and London: Routledge, 1991), pp. 33–43

Doniol-Valcroze, Jacques, 'Les Cheveux sur la soupe', *France-Observateur*, 24 April 1952

Doniol-Valcroze, Jacques, 'Déshabillage d'une petite bourgeoise sentimentale', *Cahiers du cinéma* no. 31 (January 1954), pp. 2–14

Drachline, Pierre and Claude Petit-Castelli, *Casque d'or et les Apaches* (Paris: Renaudot, 1990)

Duchen, Claire, 'Occupation housewife: The domestic ideal in 1950s France', *French Cultural Studies* 2.1/4 (1991), pp. 1–11

Duchen, Claire, *Women's Rights and Women's Lives in France 1944–1968* (London and New York: Routledge, 1994)

Dyer, Richard, *Stars*, 2nd edn (London: BFI, 1998)

Entwistle, Joanne, and Elizabeth Wilson (eds), *Body Dressing* (Oxford and New York: Berg, 2001)

Frank, Nino, 'Casque d'or par Jacques Becker', *Arts*, 1 May 1952

Fortescue, W., *The Third Republic in France 1870–1940: Conflicts and continuities* (London and New York: Routledge, 2000)

Giavarini, Laurence and Camille Taboulay, 'Becker, le Couturier', *Cahiers du cinéma* no. 454 (April 1992), pp. 60–71

Gibbs, P., 'Versatility', *Daily Telegraph*, 8 September 1952

Gledhill, Christine, 'Pleasurable negotiations' in Sue Thornham (ed.), *Feminist Film Theory: A reader* (Edinburgh: Edinburgh University Press, 1999), pp. 166–179

Grant, Elspeth, 'It's all just a wee bit squalid', *Daily Graphic*, 5 September 1952

Guilleminault, Gilbert, *Le Roman vrai de la Troisième République: La Belle Epoque* (Paris: Denoël, 1958)

Hayward, Susan, *French National Cinema* (London and New York: Routledge, 1993)

Hayward, Susan, 'Signoret's star persona and redressing the costume cinema: Jacques Becker's *Casque d'or* (1952)', *Studies in French Cinema* 4.1 (2004), pp. 15–28

Hayward, Susan, *Simone Signoret: The star as cultural sign* (London and New York: Continuum, 2004)

Hayward, Susan, 'Simone Signoret 1921–1985: The star as sign – The sign as scar' in Diana Knight and Judith Still (eds), *Women and Representation* (London: WIF, 1995), pp. 57–74

Hélie, Amélie, 'Mémoires ou histoire de Casque d'or racontée par elle-même, ou Ma Vie par Casque d'or', *Fin de siècle*, 5 June 1902, p. 1

Hewitt, Nicholas, 'Gabin, *Grisbi* and 1950s France', *Studies in French Cinema* 4.1 (2004), pp. 65–75

Hillier, Jim, *Cahiers du Cinéma: The 1950s – Neo-realism, Hollywood, New Wave* (Cambridge, Mass. Harvard University Press, 1985)

Jeancolas, Jean-Pierre, 'Beneath the despair, the show goes on: Marcel Carné's *Les Enfants du paradis* (1943–5)' in Susan Hayward and Ginette Vincendeau (eds), *French Film: Texts and contexts* (London and New York: Routledge, 2000), pp. 78–88

Jolivet, Nicole, 'Simone Signoret: Il y a vingt ans Casque d'or était en avance sur son temps', *France Soir*, 4 May 1973

Kedward, H. R. and Nancy Wood (eds), *The Liberation of France: Image and event* (Oxford: Berg, 1995)

Kirkup, James, 'Serge Reggiani: Popular actor turned singer', *Independent*, 26 July 2004, p. 34

Lambert, Gavin, 'Golden Marie', *Evening Standard*, 4 September 1952

Lambert, Gavin, 'The Movies: Casque d'or at the Academy', *New Statesman*, 13 September 1952

Lang, André, 'Les Nouveaux Films: Casque d'or', *France-Soir*, 19 April 1952

Lanoux, Armand, 'La Vraie Casque d'or' in Gilbert, Guilleminault, *Le Roman vrai de la Troisième République: La Belle Epoque* (Paris: Denoël, 1958), pp. 71–118

Laurens, Corin, '"La Femme au turban": Les femmes tondues' in H. R. Kedward and Nancy Wood (eds), *The Liberation of France: Image and event* (Oxford: Berg, 1995), pp. 155–179

Lauwick, Hervé, 'Manèges', *Noir et Blanc*, 15 February 1950

Lauwick, Hervé, 'Casque d'or', *Noir et Blanc*, 30 April 1952, p. 17

Leahy, Sarah, '"Neither charm nor sex appeal…" Just what is the appeal of Simone Signoret?', *Studies in French Cinema* 4.1 (2004), pp. 29–40

Leahy, Sarah and Susan Hayward, 'The tainted woman: Simone Signoret – site of Pathology or Agent of Retribution?' in Ulrike Sieglohr (ed.), *Heroines Without Heroes: Reconstructing female and national identities in European cinema, 1945–1951* (London and New York: Cassell, 2000), pp. 77–88

Lehmann, Andrée, *Le Rôle de la femme française au milieu du vingtième siècle*, Third edn, (Paris: Edition de la Ligue Française pour le Droit des Femmes, 1965)

Lejeune, C. A., 'No title', *Observer*, 7 September 1952

Magdalaney, Fred, '*Golden Marie*', *Daily Mail*, 5 September 1952

Magnan, Henry, 'Le Cinéma: *Casque d'or* de Jacques Becker', *Le Monde*, 18 April 1952

Malliarakis, Nikita, *Mayo: Un peintre et le cinéma* (Paris: L'Harmattan, 2002)

Mannock, P. L., 'No title', *Daily Herald*, 5 September 1952

Marie, Laurent, 'Le Chêne et le roseau: The French Communist critics and the New Wave' in Elizabeth Ezra and Sue Harris (eds), *France in Focus: Film and national identity* (Oxford and New York: Berg, 2000), pp. 43–60

McMillan, James F., *France and Women 1789–1914: Gender, society and politics* (London and New York: Routledge, 2000)

McMillan, James F., *Housewife or Harlot: The place of women in French society 1870–1940* (Brighton: Harvester Press, 1981)

Mosley, Leonard, 'No title', *Daily Express*, 29 August 1952

Mulvey, Laura, 'Visual pleasure and narrative cinema' in *Visual and Other Pleasures* (London: Macmillan, 1989), pp. 14–26

Nash, Ray, 'No title', *Star*, no date

Naumann, Claude, *Jacques Becker: Entre classicisme et modernité* (Paris: BIFI/ Durante, 2001)

Naumann, Claude, 'La Réception critique des films de Jacques Becker: première partie, de *Dernier Atout à Casque d'or*', 22 November 2002. http://www. proto.bifi.fr/ cineregards/article.asp?rub=1. Accessed 8 August 2005

Néry, Jean, '*Rue de l'Estrapade*', *Franc-Tireur*, 21 April 1953

Overby, David (ed.), *Springtime in Italy: A reader on neo-realism* (London: Talismann, 1978)

Pérez Guillermo, Gilberto, 'Jacques Becker: two films', *Sight and Sound* 38.3 (Summer 1969), pp. 142–147

Pierrot, Henriette, 'Les Sept Femmes de votre mari', *Elle*, no. 101, 21 (October 1947)

Powell, Dilys, '*Golden Marie*', *Sunday Times*, 7 September 1952

Powrie, Phil, 'Introduction: Fifteen Years of 1950s cinema', *Studies in French Cinema* 4.1 (2004), pp. 5–13

Prédal, René, *Le Cinéma français depuis 1945* (Paris: Nathan, 1991)

Quéval, Jean, '*Casque d'or*', *Radio-Cinéma-Télévision*, 4 May 1952

Quéval, Jean, 'Pavane pour apaches défunts', *Cahiers du cinéma* 3.13 (June 1952), pp. 71–72

Quéval, Jean, *Jacques Becker* (Paris: Editions Seghers, 1962)

R., D., 'No title', *Sunday Picture*, 7 September 1952

Rabourdin, Dominique and Noël Simsolo, 'Entretien avec Raymond Bussières', *Cinéma* 77 no. 219 (March 1977), pp, 34–43

Régent, Roger, '*Manèges*', *L'Epoque*, no date (article taken from CNC dossier on *Manèges*)

Rendu, Marc-Ambroise, 'La Maison de *Casque d'or* sera conservée', *Le Monde*, 21 October 1992

Alain Resnais, 'Le Bonheur au quotidien', in Claude Beylie and Freddy Buache (eds), *Jacques Becker* (Locarno: Editions du Festival de Locarno, 1991), p. 229

Rivette, Jacques and François Truffaut, 'Entretien avec Jacques Becker', *Cahiers du cinéma* no. 32 (February 1954), pp. 3–17

Rivière, Joan, 'Womanliness as a masquerade' in H. Ruitenbeek (ed.), *Psychoanalysis and Female Sexuality* (New Haven, CT: College and University Press, 1966), pp. 163–175, first published 1929

Rudorff, Raymond, *Belle Epoque: Paris in the nineties* (London: Hamish Hamilton, 1972)

Sadoul, Georges, '*Dédée d'Anvers*: Victime du poncif', *Les Lettres Françaises*, 16 September 1948, p. 6

Sadoul, Georges, 'La Haine toute nue: *Caroline chérie*, un film de Jean Anouilh, Richard Pottier et Cécil Saint-Laurent', *Les Lettres françaises*, 15 March 1951, p.6

Sadoul, Georges, 'Puissance de la sobriété: *Casque d'or*, un film français de Jacques Becker', *L'Ecran français*, 18 April 1952

Sadoul, Georges, *Ecrits I: Chroniques du cinéma français 1939–1967* (Paris: Union Générale d'Editions, 1979)

Sagner-Düchting, Karin, *Renoir: Paris and the Belle Epoque* (Munich and New York: Prestel, 1996)

Schidlow, Joshka, 'Claude Dauphin', *Télérama* no. 1507, 2 December 1978

Sellier, Geneviève, 'The Belle Epoque genre in post-war French cinema: a woman's film *à la française*?', *Studies in French Cinema* 3.1 (2003), pp. 47–53

Serge Reggiani, http://www.imdb.com/name/nm0716577. Accessed 25 May 2005

Siclier, Jacques, *La Femme dans le cinéma français* (Paris: Editions du Cerf, 1957)

Signoret, Simone, *La Nostalgie n'est plus ce qu'elle était* (Paris: Seuil, 1978)

Sim, Gregory, 'Returning to the Fold: questions of ideology in Jacques Becker's *Goupi Mains Rouges* (1942)', *French Cultural Studies* 8 (2002), pp. 5–31

Simsi, Simon, *Ciné-Passions: 7ème art et industrie de 1945 à 2000* (Paris: Dixit, 2000)

Smith, Douglas, 'A world that accords with our desires?: realism, desire and death in André Bazin's film criticism', *Studies in French Cinema* 4.2 (2004), pp. 93–102

Sorlin, Pierre, *European Cinemas, European Societies, 1939–1990* (London and New York: Routledge, 1991)

Sorlin, Pierre, *Italian National Cinema* (London and New York: Routledge, 1996)

Spade, Henri, '*Dédée d'Anvers*', *Cinémonde*, 14 September 1948

Tacchella, Jean-Charles, 'Jacques Becker: Cinéaste de toutes les générations' in Claude Beylie and Freddy Buache (eds), *Jacques Becker* (Locarno: Editions du Festival de Locarno, 1991), pp. 233–236

Tarnowski, Jean-Louis, *Essais d'esthétique et de philosophie du cinéma: pour une théorie générale de l'art cinématographique*, unpublished doctoral thesis, Université de Paris I (Lille: A.R.N.T., 1987)

Tarr, Carrie, 'Feminist Influences on the work of Yannick Bellon in the 1970s', *Studies in French Cinema* 3.1 (2003), pp. 55–65

Tobin, Yann, 'Juillet et Août en cinéma: La musique qui s'est tue', *Positif* no. 524 (October 2004), pp. 54–55

Trémois, Claude-Marie, 'Analyse d'un grand film: *Casque d'or*', *Télérama*, 30 January 1966

Truffaut, François, '*Ali Baba* et la "politique des auteurs"', *Cahiers du cinéma* no. 44 (February 1955), pp. 45–47

Truffaut, François, 'De vraies moustaches', *L'Avant scène cinéma* no. 43 (December 1964), p. 6

Truffaut, François, 'The Rogues are weary', in Jim Hillier (ed.), *Cahiers du Cinéma: The 1950s – Neo-Realism, Hollywood, New Wave* (Cambridge, Mass.: Harvard University Press, 1985), pp. 28–29.

Truffaut, François, 'Une certaine tendance du cinéma français', *Cahiers du cinéma* no. 31 (January 1954), pp. 15–29

Van Haecht, Anne, *La Prostituée: Statut et image* (Brussels: Editions de l'Université de Bruxelles, 1973)

Varennes, Henri de, 'Gazette des Tribunaux. Cour d'assises de la Seine: Casque d'or', *Le Figaro*, 31 May 1902, pp. 3–4

Vey, Jean-Louis, *Jacques Becker ou la fausse évidence* (Lyon: Aléas, 1995)

Vignaux, Valérie, *Jacques Becker ou l'exercice de la liberté* (Liège: Editions du Céfal, 2001)

Vincendeau, Ginette, 'The art of spectacle: the aesthetics of classical French cinema', in Michael Temple and Michael Witt (eds), *The French Cinema Book* (London: BFI, 2004), pp. 137–152

Vincendeau, Ginette, 'Daddy's girls: Oedipal narratives in 1930s French Films', *Iris* no. 8 (1988), pp. 70–81

Vincendeau, Ginette, *Stars and Stardom in French Cinema* (London and New York: Continuum, 2000)

Vincendeau, Ginette, *Jean-Pierre Melville: An American in Paris* (London: BFI, 2003)

Virmaux, Alain and Odette, *Le Grand Jeu et le cinéma: Anthologie* (Paris: Editions Paris Expérimental with the collaboration of the Centre National du Livre, 1996)

Whitley, Reg, 'No Title, *Daily Mirror*, 5 September 1952

Winnington, Richard, 'No Title', *News Chronicle*, 6 September 1952

Index

Index of Names

Index of Film Titles